The Mad-Doctors of Calne

Mayors and Murderer

by
Peter Carpenter

The Mad-Doctors of Calne

Mayors and Murderer

by
Peter Carpenter

Clinical Press Ltd Publishers, Bristol, United Kingdom

© *Peter Carpenter 2024*

The right of Peter Carpenter to be identified as the author and artist of this work has been asserted by him in accordance with the Copyright, Designs and Patents Act 1988.
All rights reserved. No part of this publication may be reproduced, stored in a retrieval system, or transmitted in any form or by any means, electronic, mechanical, photocopying, recording or otherwise, without prior permission from the copyright owner.
While the advice and information in this book is believed to be true and accurate at the time of going to press, neither the author, the editor, nor the publisher can accept legal responsibility for any errors or omissions that may be made. The publisher makes no warranty, express or implied, with respect to the material contained herein.

First published in the UK 2024

A catalogue record for this book is available from the British Library
ISBN: 978-1-85457- 130-4   Mad-Doctors of Calne: Mayors and Murderer by Peter Carpenter

Published by:
Clinical Press Ltd. Redland Green Farm, Redland, Bristol, BS6 7HF

Contents

List of illustrations and sources	6
Preface	7
Introduction	9
James Pownall's Family	11
James' entry to Calne	22
George Shadforth Ogilive	26
Calne Asylum	30
James' success in Calne	43
James Pownall, Mad-doctor	46
Ogilvie in Bristol: Ridgeway House and its destruction.	53
James' 1854 bout of insanity	73
James' 1859 bout of insanity	81
In Northwoods Asylum	87
The dispute over discharge	91
Discharge and murder	102
The Murder	107
Arrest, trial and reactions	110
The Commissioners change policy	122
The public reaction	123
James' Life as a Criminal Lunatic	125
The lives of the other Players	131
Reflections	137
Appendix 1 - George Ogilvie's patients at Northfield House	141
Appendix 2 – James Pownall's Patients at Northfield House	151
Appendix 3 – The Broadmoor case notes for James Pownall.	156
Bibliography	164

List of Illustrations:

Figure 1: James Pownall's examination record at Apothecaries Hall 22
Figure 2: 30 The Green - the house behind it was part of the house. 28
Figure 3: The Memorial window. 29
Figure 4: St Mary the Virgin, Calne - the memorial window is in the foreground 29
Figure 5: Calne in 1840 from the Tithe Map 30
Figure 6: Northfield House 33
Figure 7: Northfield House from the back 35
Figure 8: James Pownall in the 1850s from a family photograph 50
Figure 9: James Signs his oath of Office - from Minutes of Borough of Calne 52
Figure 10: Ridgeway House 53
Figure 11: Mr Purnell Bransby Purnell, Chief Magistrate of Gloucestershire 55
Figure 12: Modern image of Sussex House, by the River Thames. 78
Figure 13: Northwoods Asylum 87
Figure 14: The silver urn and table presented to Purnell 89

Sources of Illustrations:

Figure 1: Permission of Worshipful Company of Apothecaries

Figure 2; Figure 3; Figure 4; Figure 6 – photos by author

Figure 5: see website KnowYourPlace reproduced permission of Wiltshire & Swindon Heritage Centre [WSHC]

Figure 7: Reproduced with permission of archivist, St Marys School.

Figure 8: In collection of descendants of James through sister Mary Britton. Reproduced with permission of family. Evidence for ascription not known.

Figure 9: Permission of WSHC. ref: G18/100/1

Figure 10: Bristol Central Reference Library reproduced with permission.

Figure 11: Shire Hall, Gloucester, reproduced with kind permission from Gloucestershire County Council

Figure 12: https://commons.wikimedia.org/w/index.php?curid=35873610; By Edwardx - Own work, CC BY-SA 3.0. reproduced under Creative Commons Licence.

Figure 13: In Public Domain: https://wellcomecollection.org/works/p6rbpksh.

Figure 14: Copyright Victoria and Albert Museum – reproduced with permission

Preface

Calne is a small, picturesque Wiltshire town in the South West of England. Although only ever having had a small population it has had some historically famous inhabitants. It was in Calne around the year 978 that Dunstan, the Archbishop of Canterbury, met the King's Council (the Witenagemot) and justified his reorganisation of the national church. This was challenged until, supposedly at Dunstan's miraculous instigation, part of the building collapsed killing his opponents. Dunstan later became a popular saint!

Natural philosopher (scientist, in modern terminology) Joseph Priestley discovered oxygen in 1774 whilst working at Bowood House, just a couple of miles outside of Calne. He had already, in 1772, demonstrated that plants provided the "air" needed for a candle to burn or a mouse to breathe. In 1779, also in Calne, Jan Ingen Housz, a Dutch scientist, doctor and botanist, immersed plants in water in sunlight and in shade. He demonstrated that small bubbles of gas were given off in daylight but not in the dark and was able to prove that the gas was oxygen. Housz had discovered photosynthesis.

From 1814 to 1816 Samuel Taylor Coleridge, poet and writer of *The Rime of the Ancient Mariner* and *Kubla Khan: or A Vision in a Dream,* lived in Calne, renting a house in Church Street owned by the surgeon George Page. Coleridge's highly successful play "Remorse" was performed in Calne.

This book, however, is not about these illustrious Calne doyens. Their stories have been told elsewhere. The bad and the mad are equally as interesting, so instead of the famous residents, it is about an infamously insane mad-doctor from Calne and another doctor whose life was interwoven with the mad-doctor. Read on….

Introduction

This is an account of one of the most notorious doctors of Calne, James Pownall. He was the son of a Jamaican freed woman and trained and worked in Calne as a successful Surgeon. Medical doctors who looked after insane patients were known as Mad-Doctors and he ran a Lunatic Asylum at Northfield House. Pownall was twice elected to be a town councillor and elected mayor in 1853. However he had a secret – he had bouts of insanity when he thought his food poisoned, tried to kill himself and assaulted people around him…. he was sometimes quite insanely mad!

James Pownall spent time in private lunatic asylums but was able to build his practice in Calne. He assaulted one of his patients and shot another but the events were smoothed over and he was never prosecuted for these events. The authorities supervising the Asylum avoided all publicity on the matter. He then almost killed his 86 year old mother-in-law and went again into Northwoods private Asylum in Frampton Cotterell, near Bristol. He was discharged as having recovered but soon after killed a maid. He ended up in the Broadmoor Criminal Lunatic Asylum until he died, whilst the events were raked over in public and the key official players vied to transfer blame.

Such is the story of our man, and the story of this book, but it is a story that is closely intertwined with that of another Calne character, his wife's brother-in-law and his medical partner, George Ogilvie. Ogilvie was successful in Calne and looked after the family when James was insane. He was worried about James' release but could not get the magistrates to agree as they had suffered a previous run-in with him that ruined his business and sullied his reputation with them.

Introduction

James' story reflects some of the tensions of the time: how as a man of status James was allowed to avoid prosecution until he killed; the enormous fear of wrongful detention in private asylums; and the debate on who determined when a lunatic should be free to leave an asylum.

As an asylum doctor who himself went insane and was a Victorian insane murderer, his case has been described by several people[1] but not at length. I recently wrote a paper about Pownall[2] but realised that a bigger picture needed to be described. This book is an attempt to describe both the story of the man, his relatives, the people around him and the society he operated in. In this book I have tried to give the fullest story possible.

This short book could not have been written without the help and support of many people. Firstly Deric Brewer, who allowed me to continue my preoccupation with this case, Sue Boddington of the Calne Heritage Centre who looked through the Calne records for me, Jill Britton who helped me with some of James' background and the family photograph; Angelo Harrison and Elizabeth Christie who helped me with information on Northfield House, and Paul and Lois Goddard for their editorial assistance. Thank you all.

References

1. D J Vaughan. Mad or Bad. Barnsley: Pen & Sword, 2017; Tomkins A. Mad doctors? The significance of medical practitioners admitted as patients to the first English county asylums up to 1890. History of Psychiatry. 2012;23(4):437-453; John Osbourne has transcribed the newspaper reports at the time for Calne Heritage Centre: http://www.calneheritage.co.uk/2019/07/calnes-dr-pownall-and-murder-of-louisa.html;

2. P.Carpenter (2022). "The case of Dr Pownall – mad doctor, sane patient and insane murderer." History of Psychiatry 33(2): 200-216

James Pownall's Family

James Pownall's paternal grandfather was from North-west England. William Pownall was born in 1740 to a well established family in Wilmslow, Cheshire, where another branch had an ancestral home, Pownall Hall which is now used as a school.[1] He married and became a merchant and grocer in nearby Macclesfield. He left Macclesfield possibly to get away from his wife's family, the Cornes, who were becoming Catholic supporters and converts. He came to Bristol, rather than Liverpool where other relatives were, and is there by 1782. He probably went to Bristol as it had a strong non-conformist leaning as after a few years he and his wife were baptised there as Moravians.[2]

He did not do well in Bristol financially as he twice went through bankruptcy proceedings.[3] Trade abroad was risky and even when the goods got here there could be problems: a promissory note of his to the Customs at Milford Haven was once stolen:

> On the night of Thursday 24th July [1800] ... the Customs House at the Port of Milford in the County of Pembroke, was feloniously broken open by some Person or Persons. .. who forced open the Desks of the Collector and Comptroller with a Sawyer's Axe and stole thereout cash ... amounting to ... Three Hundred and Sixty-four Pounds and upwards, and One Bill drawn by William Pownal of Bristol, at One Month after Date, on Messrs. Goobehere, Wigan & Co. London, for the sum of Thirty Six Pounds, in favour of George Hough, the Collector of Customs at the said Port of Milford.
>
> [Any of the offenders who 'discover' the others, will be pardoned].[4]

We do not know what he was trading in as a grocer – Milford was a whaling port and a grocer would be selling whaling products but Milford would also have taken trade from Ireland as well as sugar and coffee from the Caribbean.

William retired to Macclesfield as a Moravian minister after his second bankruptcy, and died there in 1828 supported by an annuity from his son.[5]

James' father, James Corne Pownall [who I will call James Corne for clarity from his son James] was born in 1776 in Macclesfield but grew up with his parents in Bristol where he was baptised in Temple Church.[6] He trained as a lawyer and emigrated to Jamaica.

Why he chose to leave for Jamaica is not clear but it was still a place to make one's fortune and going there both escaped the pressure to join the military during the wars with France and avoided the local family consequences of his father's first bankruptcy. William Pownall does not appear to have had any estates in Jamaica but he was almost certainly trading with the dominion and must have had links for James Corne to exploit - certainly William's daughter Elizabeth became intimately linked with families involved in the Jamaica trade.

Jamaica was still one of the wealthiest dominions of England: a place that made many wealthy but where tropical disease killed frequently. Many plantation owners lived in England and employed others to run their estates. The British who arrived could make money and themselves become plantation owners.

James Corne did well in Jamaica and became an established member of ruling society there: He was Deputy Adjutant General in the local Militia, an elected representative in the Jamaica House of Assembly in 1815[7] and afterwards Chief Justice for the Court of Common Pleas in Jamaica.[8] He became a member and then assistant judge of the Supreme Court of Judicature.[9] He supervised estates for their absentee owners and himself bought estates and enslaved people. In 1823 he owns 125 enslaved people on his estate at Silver Hill in St Andrews parish, 8 in another and in addition acts as the attorney for the estates of others, controlling about another 400 enslaved people.[10] There are several newspaper adverts for escaped or apprehended 'slaves' that he claims to own or be the 'trustee' for.

His main estate seems to have been Silver Hill, which he owned by 1809. Assuming it was by Silver Hill Mountain above Kingston, he grew coffee as sugar was grown generally on the coastal plains – he also acquired Stepney Lodge estate by 1815, and as he left this to the mother of his children this may have been where some of them grew up.

He was part of the Anglican Church, where all his children were baptised. Interestingly his speech against using state money to rebuild a presbyterian chapel has survived[11] as has his support for the slave registration bill of 1816.[12]

He died of typhus in Jamaica on 4 September 1825.[13] His gravestone is in St Andrews Churchyard and is recorded as saying:[14]

> SACRED
> TO THE MEMORY OF
> JAMES CORNE POWNELL, ESQ.,
> PROPRIETOR OF SILVER HILL
> PLANTATION
> ONE OF THE ASSEMBLY
> OF THE SUPREME COURT OF JAMAICA,
> AND A MEMBER OF THE
> HONORABLE HOUSE OF ASSEMBLY.
> HE DEPARTED THIS LIFE
> ON THE 4th DAY OF SEPTEMBER, 1823,
> AGED 49 YEARS.

Few men arrived in Jamaica with wives from England and few relatives visited. It was the custom for white men to take non-white women as 'concubines' or 'housekeepers'. The enslaved state of children was always determined by that of the mother. If a man sired children from one of their enslaved women, the parish church did not record the colour of her skin, just the names of the parents, but if the woman was not enslaved the parish registers duly registered that the woman was free and if either of the parents were coloured. There was in theory a whole classification of racial interbreeding similar to that in Brazil: people were classified as mullato [half white], quadroon [three quarter white], mustee and mustifino. It is said that only the mustifino, one sixteenth black, were considered legally white. However the Jamaican registers often label the same person Mullato or Quadroon or Mustee so it is clear the rectors were not interested in exploring genealogy and suggests that the racial-mix classifications did not determine how children were treated by their fathers. The terminology probably was used to indicate how a person looked rather than their forebears.

There was a quite large group of free coloured women. They usually had to work and often ran lodging houses or acted as housekeepers or partners/concubines for the Europeans. But they had little security unless they owned property in their own right. Some did gain plantations and owned enslaved people, often through their 'husbands'.

Social convention did not allow marriage between the planters and their concubines but many men recognised their offspring as their legitimate children and took them back with them when they returned to Britain. This also occurred in other European colonies.[15] As a result there was quite a sizeable group of financially comfortable people in England who were of mixed heritage, though their heritage is rarely mentioned once they were in England.

James Corne had a 25 year relationship with his 'housekeeper' Sarah Watt, a 'free mulatto' or 'quadroon'[16] or 'free woman of colour'.[17] He fathered at least 10 children by Sarah and they are the only children acknowledged in his will. In his will he left Sarah a lifetime annuity of 150 Jamaican pounds (and in a codicil, all his recently acquired estates and slaves) and names 7 living children, all by Sarah. Sarah became the owner of Stepney Lodge estate in St Andrews along with the house contents and in 1835 claimed £754 compensation for her

38 enslaved persons on Stepney Lodge and possibly also for some on a Clarendon estate.[18] She probably owned enslaved people before James Corne's death.[19] She never left Jamaica. She died in 1837 and was buried next to James Corne, though with a minimal epitaph:[20]

'Mrs Sarah Watt died 3 March 1837 aged 56'.

In his will James Corne put his main Silver Hill estate in trust to provide both for Sarah and the support and education of his children in England. In addition he gave an annuity of £100 for his father and then after William's death for his sister, Sarah Birchall Pownall, living in Bristol.[21]

When the will was made James Pownall was probably already an apprentice surgeon. The will directs that James is not to reside in Jamaica (presumably as he might still be treated as non-white) and that James' sisters are to lose their inheritance if they return to Jamaica unless brought there by their husbands – presumably to get them away from the risk of themselves becoming concubines.

James Corne's estate was finally wound up in 1844 when all the children reached full age.[22] The English trustees of his will were his older sister Elizabeth and two Bristol Merchants: Robert Lewis of Cleeve Lodge in Downend who was a merchant and ship owner running ships to the States. Lewis had Wesleyan sympathies as he left £500 to a Wesleyan preacher.[23] The other trustee was Robert Bright, a 30 year old, up and coming son of an ex-master of the Merchant Venturers and partner in the trading and ship owning company of Gibbs & Bright of Liverpool and Bristol, who himself claimed for enslaved people in Barbados and who clearly traded with Jamaica. His family were Unitarian in leaning. He himself was a Merchant Venturer and later chair of the Bristol Free Port Association and a mover in the development of Avonmouth docks. His firm bought the SS Great Britain in 1850.[24]

We do not know if James Corne visited England and met the male executors or relied on the written word of his sister. Neither male executor seems to have been related to the Pownalls but were active and wealthy traders whose non-conformity leanings and shipping trade probably put them in contact with the family.

James Corne Pownall's siblings

Many of William Pownall's children became intimately linked to trade with the Dominions and many seem rather colourful characters. However we have no evidence that they supported James when he was adult.

James Corne's only brother the **Rev. Augustus William Pownall** is a bit of a mystery. He was probably the eldest, born about 1772 but his baptism record has not been found. He probably did not travel to Bristol with his parents as in the 1790s he was in business in Shrewsbury where his mother's relatives lived.[25] When staying in Bristol with his parents on 1st March 1800 he, as a 'gentleman from Shrewsbury' married Sarah Allen, a spinster, by licence at St James in Bristol. She was illiterate and none of his family attended. Why they wanted or needed to get married is not recorded but for such a social mismatch one must assume she was pregnant or possibly he married someone who would go to Jamaica with him. Unfortunately the vicar adds a footnote dated a week later:

> 8th March: It was discovered a short time after this marriage took place that this woman's name was not Allen but Wallace & that she was then and is now the wife of Henry Wallace, a mariner on board his Majesty's ship Beaulieu.

Her maiden name was Clay and she had married Wallace in 1798. There is no record of her prosecution for bigamy which would have caused great embarrassment to Augustus. He ended the Shrewsbury business partnership and emigrated to Jamaica where he became the Rector of St David's. In 1811 he married a plantation heiress, Mary Lowe.

However he became an absentee rector after 1815 and in 1817 was dismissed from the post, an event that reached the English newspapers.[26] He died in Jamaica in 1821.[27]

His only surviving adult child, the Revd William Lowe Pownall, married cousin Hannah, James Corne's daughter, but he later ran off with another woman and bigamously married her.[28]

James Corne's older sister **Elizabeth Corne Pownall**, born 1774, moved to Bristol with her parents and also became linked to Jamaica. In 1802, at the mature age of twenty-eight she married William Bennett, aged twenty-five.[29] They had three daughters and he became a mature student at Oxford in 1805. William appears to have had independent money – he left his children £1500 to divide amongst them at marriage and his wife an annuity to be reduced if she remarried.[30] In his marriage notice he is 'of Norfolk' but the Oxford records state his father William was of Westminster. He left a small annuity to his childhood nurse who lived in Denver by Downham Market. Unfortunately with such a common name it is difficult to learn more about them but there is a Bennett family in Jamaica. William fell ill and died in 1807 on a voyage to Jamaica either to see his brother-in-law or relatives' estates. James Corne was trustee and executor for his will along with a London Solicitor.

Two years after William's death, Elizabeth married Charles Mais, a widowed Bristol born 'Hat Manufacturer' and merchant with history. He had made his fortune in Jamaica where he fathered five children by a 'free mulatto' or 'quadroon', Ann Ivey. He returned to Bristol in 1793 with his five Jamaican children (but without Ann Ivey), and then married twice and had a further son. Elizabeth was his third wife. One of his Jamaican sons, Jeremiah Mais, a Customs officer, married Elizabeth's daughter Emmeline Corne Bennett. Two of his other Jamaican sons became clergymen and the fourth a headmaster. Jeremiah and his brother the Rev John Mais became trustees for the estate of James Corne Pownall's daughter Mary Ann, when she married.

Elizabeth seems to have been very close to James Corne – she was an executor of his will and James left annuities for all of her children on the same terms as his own except that they were to have half that of his children. It is reasonable to assume that James Corne's children lived with Elizabeth when they were sent to England.

James Corne Pownall's only other sister, **Sarah Birchall Pownall** lived in Bristol and died a spinster in 1847.

James Corne Pownall's children

We only know of the 10 children James Corne had by Sarah Watt. There is no record of him fathering enslaved children by his enslaved women so he may have been faithful to Sarah. Though three sons were baptised, only James reached adulthood as did five daughters:

Mary Ann Pownall, born 1809, married John Britton, a 'Gentleman and Grazier', in Westbury on Trym, where her Aunt Elizabeth lived and where she later lived. John came from a well established family in Corston, where he and Mary were eventually buried. They emigrated to New York in 1835 for 20 years and in 1850 are living in Elbridge by Syracuse, where he is a teacher. She had at least five children, four of whom were born in New York. At her marriage, her money from James Corne was put in a trust, and the abuse of this trust triggered litigation, the stress of which brought on a bout of James' insanity.

Jane Lewis Pownall, born 1812, who married a barrister, Edward Chester Jones in 1846 from her brother's house in Calne. She had three children in London where she died in 1892. We have no evidence her husband was later involved legally in James' case but he must have given advice at times.

Hannah Pownall, who married her cousin the Rev William Lowe Pownall. The marriage probably ended after a decade as in 1851 she is living apart from him as a married governess. William proceeded to have thirteen children by Eleanor Robertson, moving to be a clergyman in Ireland to avoid the family. He bigamously married Eleanor in London whilst Hannah was still alive. Hannah moved to live with her sister, Isabella, and died in Switzerland.

Sarah Pownall lived as a spinster of independent means, often staying with her siblings, until she died in 1898.

Isabella Pownall, another spinster of independent means, lived with her brother and sisters until she married in 1864.

The experience of this family was that being genetically 'of colour' was not necessarily a penalty in England. None of the records in England refer to the person being of colour or of mixed race, though it is described in the Jamaican parish registers where colour mattered to God.

One example of this is John Mais,[31] a man 'of colour', who married Phillipina, the daughter of a 'free mullato'. John and Phillipina emigrated to England, where they were successful merchants. One of their sons Charles Mais, was an apprentice surgeon at the Bristol Infirmary, paying £300 for his place, but died young in 1823 – interestingly Richard Smith the senior Infirmary surgeon who relates the detailed story of Charles says he was born on 3 April 1803 in Jamaica but does not mention that he is 'of colour' though he does say that the oddest thing about him was that he had never been to London![32]

Given James's later mental illness, it's worthwhile looking for a family history of illness. There is little evidence but at the time it was possible that an insane or intellectually disabled child or adult could be kept in the family home and so out of official records and invisible to us. The only hint of insanity is in the descendants of Charles Mais – the son of his second wife entered an asylum when 60; and two of his children by Elizabeth died in asylums. These entered at a younger age and stayed until they died at an advanced age, which may indicate a long term condition such as an intellectual disability. However their death certificates mention only senile decay. Such things were kept off the official records.

It is interesting to remember that the Mais family were originally hat manufacturers and that between the 18th and 20th century UK hat makers used large amounts of mercury in the process. This led to the phrase "mad as a hatter" due to heavy metal poisoning causing insanity. Luckily the use of mercury in this way stopped in 1941 because the dangers were recognised.

References

1. See J Burke: A Genealogical and Heraldic history of the Commoners of Great Britain and Ireland... Vol 4, London Henry Colburn 1838. P18: Pownall family tree. The Liverpool branch had William Pownall who was mayor of Liverpool 1767 and the grandson inherited Pownall Hall.
2. See genealogy search sites. His wife was baptised at the same time in 1791.
3. See London Gazette 29 Mar 1796 p307 when he gets his certificate of discharge; and 12 June 1810 p875 when he is again taken to the bankruptcy court.
4. London Gazette 13 Aug 1800 p962. 'Custom House August 23, 1800'
5. His son bequeathed him £100 a year suggesting he was more impoverished after he retired, either from lack of income or from distributing his wealth.
6. Baptised 28 Feb 1790 Temple Church: James Corn Pownall born 29 Jan 1776 son Wm Pownall & Sarah Birchall. The vicar of Temple Church, Joseph Easterbrook was a friend of John Wesley who often preached at Temple Church.
7. Royal Gazette of Jamaica 4 Nov 1815
8. Chester Chronicle 25 November 1825 p2
9. In 1817 Jamaica Almanac civil lists.
10. National Archives: Office of Registry of Colonial Slaves and Slave Compensation Commission: Records
11. Royal Gazette of Jamaica supplement vol38 from 14 Dec to 21 Dec 1816 p1-2 'Proceedings in the Honourable House of Assembly'
12. Royal Gazette of Jamaica additional postscript vol38 from 30 Nov to 7 Dec 1816 p1 'From the Kingston Chronicle'
13. Bristol Mirror: Death notice 5 Nov 1825
14. Lawrence-Archer, J. H. (James Henry), Monumental inscriptions of the British West Indies from the earliest date .. London: Chatto & Windus. 1875 page 257
15. See for example: Petley C. Boundaries of Rule, Ties of Dependency: Jamaican Planters, Local Society and the Metropole, 1800 – 1834. PhD Thesis, Univ Warwick Dept History, 2003; Trahey, E. (2019). Among Her Kinswomen: Legacies of Free Women of Color in Jamaica. The William and Mary Quarterly 76(2), 257-288. Thomas C. Holt. The problem of freedom: race, labour, and politics in Jamaica and Britain, 1832- 1938 (Baltimore) 1992 and Meleisa Ono-George 'To Be despised': Discourses of Sexual-Economic Exchange in Nineteenth-Century Jamaica c1780- 1890. PhD Thesis. Univ Warwick Dept History. 2014
16. Jamaica, Church of England Parish Register Transcripts, 1664-1880: bapt 15 April 1801, 'William the son of Sarah Watt, a quadroon woman, by James Cawn Pownall.'
17. Jamaica, Church of England Parish Register Transcripts, 1664-1880: from bapt 7/4/1824 of three children aged 6 to 6 months
18. See UCL slavery website https://www.ucl.ac.uk/lbs/claim/view/17563
19. See UCL slavery website cited above
20. The St Andrew parish register notes the burial of a "Watt" with no other details, in the churchyard on 6 March 1837. The book Lawrence-Archer, J. H. (James Henry), Monumental inscriptions of the British West Indies from the earliest date .. London: Chatto & Windus. 1875 page 257 records a 'Mrs

Sarah Watt ob 3 March 1837 aged 56' immediately preceding James' [I am grateful to Jill Britton for directing me to this]
21. National Archives Prob 11/1719/375 Will James Corne Pownall proved P.C.C. 20 Dec 1826.
22. See The London Gazette 28 June 1844 p2233 for notice of wind up.
23. Alive 1746-1840. See his will proved in Prerogative Court of Canterbury and book by Rev Arthur E. Jones Our Parish Mangotsfield...1899 reprint 1978 by Kingsmead Press, Bath. Also various histories of Bristol by Latimer.
24. See Patrick McGrath: The Merchant Venturers of Bristol: A History of the Society of Merchant Venturers of the City of Bristol from its origin to the present day. Bristol :The Society of Merchant Venturers. 1975.
25. The London Gazette 19 Aug 1800 p955 has notice of voluntary dissolution on 8 March of his partnership with Thos Baker and John Baker as the firm of Thomas Baker, Son and Pownall. We do not know what the trade of the firm was.
26. See London Courier and Evening Gazette 11 Dec 1817.p2 'From the Jamaica Papers'
27. Buried 9 April 1821 St Davids, Jamaica [see p90 of register]
28. He lived with and had 13 children by Eleanor Robertson, living mainly in Ireland. He married her as a 'widower' when Hannah was still alive. [Information from Jill Britton]
29. Marriage notice Gloucester Journal 3 May 1802 p3 – at St James Church, Bristol. William Bennett Esq of the County of Norfolk to Miss Pownall daughter of Mr Pownall of Bristol. Marriage deed shows her parents were present.
30. See his will Prerogative Court of Canterbury
31. He was probably the natural son of Charles Mais's brother Henry.
32. See Bristol Archives – 35893/36/I_i. Richard Smith Memoirs vol 12 page 584.

James' entry to Calne

James Pownall was born and baptised in Jamaica in 1807.[1] He would have spent his early childhood in St Andrews parish with his mother on either Stepney Lodge where his mother probably lived, or on the Silver Hill estate, but then, like his sisters, was sent to England probably under the care of his aunt Elizabeth Mais. We do not know how old he was when he left his mother, but he was probably educated in one of the many private schools in Bristol.

From his father's legacies James had financial support until he was twenty-one and was able to access up to £1000 to set himself up in business. His father had not been so wealthy that he could live a life of leisure. In 1823, when he was about 16, he was apprenticed to George Shadforth Ogilvie, surgeon in Calne, in Wiltshire, and presumably James Corne paid his fees. As part of his required studies he also spent nine months at the 'Central Infirmary' in London and attended four courses of lectures in London.[2]

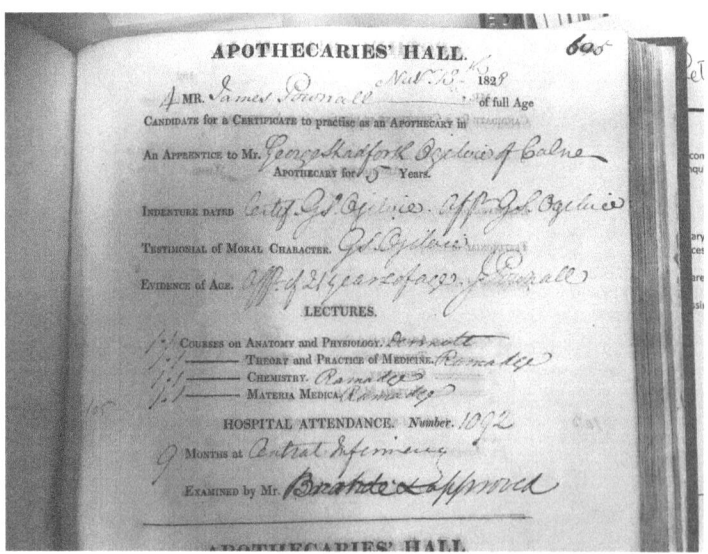

Figure 1: James Pownall's examination record at Apothecaries Hall

At this time – in the 1820s and after – medicine had started to evolve as a profession separate from quackery. Traditionally there were three types of practitioner – the Apothecary, Surgeon and Physician. The Apothecaries were the lowest status – they were officially meant to dispense medication only to the prescription of a Physician, but after a court case, most prescribed and so serviced the poorer echelons of society. The Surgeons were of middle status. They could break skin and operate though this was still a time of poor hygiene and no anaesthetic so surgery happened *in extremis*. Both surgeons and apothecaries were usually trained by apprenticeship but there was no central licensing system or regulated training. As a result it was easy to practice with minimal training until in 1815 the Apothecaries Act had required all Apothecaries to be licensed by the Worshipful Company of Apothecaries in London who started to impose training requirements similar to those of surgeons. It quickly became the rule for budding doctors to gain both the exams for Membership of the Royal College of Surgeons, MRCS, and Licentiate of the Society of Apothecaries, LSA, and be qualified as a Surgeon-Apothecary. These became the General Practitioners of society. They were generally seen as tradesmen, and few had a high income but in small towns they were held with respect. The third group was the Physician – a man with a medical degree – M.D. – who took your history and examined but rarely touched and never broke the skin. They claimed to be the best doctor to see, and presented themselves as cultured gentlemen, suitable for seeing the higher echelons of society for a handsome fee. They prescribed but did not make up medications or operate. They were in theory regulated by the Royal College of Physicians but the provinces were difficult to regulate and in the past bishops could also licence someone to be a physician. They tried to insist they were in charge of the other branches of the profession but there were few physicians in the provinces and the surgeon-apothecary gained his own independent status though most still aspired to become physicians.

At this time Calne was a small Wiltshire market town, originally a Saxon king's estate but which had developed into a wealthy cloth making town with a market servicing the countryside around. The main toll road from London to Bath and Bristol ran through it, so frequent passing coaches added to its wealth. It had seen a spur canal built to serve it by 1810 but the cloth making was running down, ceasing by 1850. In 1821 it had a population of about 3500 and grew only by 15% over the next 60 years. It did, however become a municipal borough in 1835 with its own mayor and town court and by the 1851 Census there were at least six doctors living there.[3] It was of sufficient historical status to send two M.P.s to parliament. There was an established Methodist chapel there by 1811 and a Quaker meeting house in 1829. The religious affiliations may explain why George was there. Why James was placed with George is unknown but it was probably as he was available, and the fees were suitable, though it is possible the Methodist and Moravian families led to a connection though both George and James appear to have been Anglicans as adults.

As an apprentice James would have lived with George and his wife on the Green in Calne so he could be called to help at any time. This obviously brought him into contact with their relatives and in August 1828 as he reached 21, he married Ann Lucretia Bishop,[4] the younger sister of George's wife, Bridget. As she reached 21 she came into her £1200 legacy from her fathers will. With his apprenticeship completed and requisite studies performed, James Pownall of Calne was then examined for and obtained his M.R.C.S. [Member of the Royal College of Surgeons] and L.S.A. [Licentiate of the Society of Apothecaries] in November 1828[5] and started practice with all the requisite national qualifications needed to operate as a general medical practitioner - a Surgeon Apothecary.

References

1. "Jamaica, Church of England Parish Register Transcripts, 1664-1880," Registrar General's Department, Spanish Town. database with images, FamilySearch (https://familysearch.org/ark:/61903/3:1:939F-8FKW-J?cc=1827268&wc=M6GG-MTL%3A161383201%2C161404801 : 20 May 2014), Kingston > Baptisms 1793-1825, Vol. 2 > image 95 of 228; bapt 14 July 1807 aged about 5 months.
2. From the certificate of his examination at the Worshipful Company of Apothecaries in 1828.
3. See Norman Beale: Is that the Doctor? A History of the Calne GPs. Calne, Norman Beale 1998.
4. Hampshire Chronicle 18 Aug 1828. James' residence is given as Stowe, Gloucestershire [by St Braivels] in the newspapers but as Stone, Gloucestershire in the Sarum Marriage licence allegation so almost certainly a misprint in the newspapers. In the marriage certificate he states he is of Calne.
5. He gained his LSA on 13 Nov 1828 when of Calne. [Apothecaries register: 605: apprentice to GS Ogilvie apothecary for 5 years, who gives testimonial for moral character. He attended lectures from [Francis] Ramadge [M.D.] who famously sued the Lancet for Libel [and got a farthing] – he attended the 'Central infirmary' for 9 months, and [George Derby] Dermott, who taught at the Medical School in Soho.

George Shadforth Ogilive

George Shadforth Ogilvie was 9 years older than James, born on the Isle of Man in 1791. His father John Ogilvie was from Scotland and had become a Wesleyan Itinerant Minister, entering the ministry in 1782 and moving around Scotland and the North, either filling in for ministers or acting as a missionary around the country. He probably met his wife when he was preaching on the Isle of Man in 1785 and returned to marry Catherine Corrin there in 1787[1] and in 1791 when George was baptised. George must have had a very nomadic childhood as John continued to move frequently. John's placements moved southwards[2] and he ended up in Cornwall where he semi-retired in 1821 and died in Duloe, Cornwall in 1839.[3]

George's younger brother, Charles Atmore Ogilvie, like his brother was named after a fellow Wesleyan Minister, but was re-baptised as an Anglican at age 18 and became a reputed high church Anglican as well as the vicar of Duloe and Rector of Ross-on-Wye.[4]

George's only sister Eleanor Corrin Ogilvie never married, living with her brothers until she died in 1860.

George acquired his Membership of the Royal College of Surgeons in 1812 when he was 21. There is little documentation for his Surgeon's examination so we do not know who he trained under but he did not formally qualify as an apothecary, which only became necessary with the 1815 Apothecaries Act. He appears to have first set up in Bradford-on-Avon as in 1818 'Mr Ogilvie, Surgeon of Bradford' is quoted on a case of food poisoning.[5] He married Bridget Bishop in Calne in 1820 when she was 21 and had come into her father's bequest of £1200 and then set up his business there. He is registered in the local rates taking over a house in Church Street in February 1821 immediately after he married.[6]

Bridget Bishop came from an established Calne family. Her grandfather was a yeoman and her father a land-owning 'gentleman'. The family owned land in the Northfield area and probably built

Northfield House where the widowed mother lived. Under the terms of their father's will, the sisters received £1200 from their father's estate on reaching twenty-one. Both married when twenty-one and the money must have been helpful in setting up their husbands' businesses.

Bridget's younger brother John Dommett Bishop was 8 when George married into the family and was probably inspired by George to train as a Surgeon Apothecary He trained at Guys Hospital in London, obtained his MRCS LSA in 1836 and practiced in Stoke Newington in London. He returned to Calne in the 1850's, ostensibly to retire after an injury. He soon re-entered practice and became an important doctor within Calne, becoming mayor five times.

Bridget's younger sister Anne Lucretia Bishop, usually called Lucretia, married James Pownall. Bridget's youngest sister, Julia married Richard Hodgson Smyth who was born a Quaker, and worked variously as a warehouseman and merchant. For a time they lived by her brother John in Stoke Newington and their children were baptised as Methodists. Richard then was the 'Proprietor of Panorama of an Overland Route to California at Egyptian Hall',[7] a touring moving panorama that was also shown in Manchester[8] and advertised thus:[9]

CALIFORNIA and its GOLD MINES—
FREMONT'S overland ROUTE to OREGON, TEXAS, and CALIFORNIA, across the Rocky Mountains, made by the United States Government, Illustrated by a grand MOVING PAINTING from Washington City, portraying the thrilling scenes that occurred to Colonel Fremont and party, and Sir William Drummond Stewart and party, while crossing the Rocky Mountains, and discovery of the Great Gold Mines, is now OPEN for PUBLIC EXHIBITION at the EGYPTIAN HALL, Piccadilly, and exhibiting every Afternoon, at Half-past Two; Evenings, at a Quarter to Eight. — Admission 1s.; Stalls, 2s.; Amphitheatre, 6d.

They then moved to Concord by Sydney, New South Wales where two sons died. Julia is back in England in 1881 as a widow and died in 1887 in Westbury-on-Trym.

Figure 2: 30 The Green in 2023 - the house behind it was part of the house.

After marrying, George and Bridget soon moved to what is now "30 The Green" in Calne where their three children were born.

- Mary Ellen Ogilvie born in 1823 who remained single and lived with her father until he died and then married William Gilder the vicar of Mackworth in Derbyshire. They soon retired to Margate where she was widowed and then died in 1899.
- Kate Ogilvie, born in 1825, who also remained unmarried and living with her father until at least 1861, when she disappears from English records and may have gone to live with her brother in South Africa.
- George Ogilvie, born 1826, matriculated at Wadham College,

Oxford in 1855 and became a Canon in 1862. He appears to have been Headmaster at a Grammar school in 'Buenos Ayres' before moving to Cape Town in 1858 where he was Headmaster of St George Grammar School. In 1861 he introduced the game of Rugby Union to his school, the Diocesan College in Cape Town. It is said to be still called GOG's game in South Africa.[10] He rose to be the Vice-Chancellor of the University of the Cape of Good Hope from 1895.[11]

Bridget died in 1829 and George never remarried. He had a memorial window installed, facing their house in the Chapel of St Edmund in the Parish Church of St Mary the Virgin where they worshipped.

Figure 4:
St Mary the Virgin, Calne - the memorial window is in the foreground by the doorway.

He moved into Northfield House in Curzon Street, and lived there with his mother-in-law, Bridget Bishop who presumably helped look after his children (though they soon went to boarding schools). He operated his surgical practice from the house. George continued to do well in Calne and was well regarded. He became a Burgess (Alderman) of the Town and was Mayor in 1840 and Alderman from May 1842, until at least 1844.[12]

Calne Asylum

George bought Northfield House from Bridget Bishop and from 1833 to 1845 licensed it as a lunatic asylum, for up to seven patients.[13] George is the only name on the licence, but James later told the Visitors that he had been a partner in the business. He was certainly a partner in the General Practice part of the business.

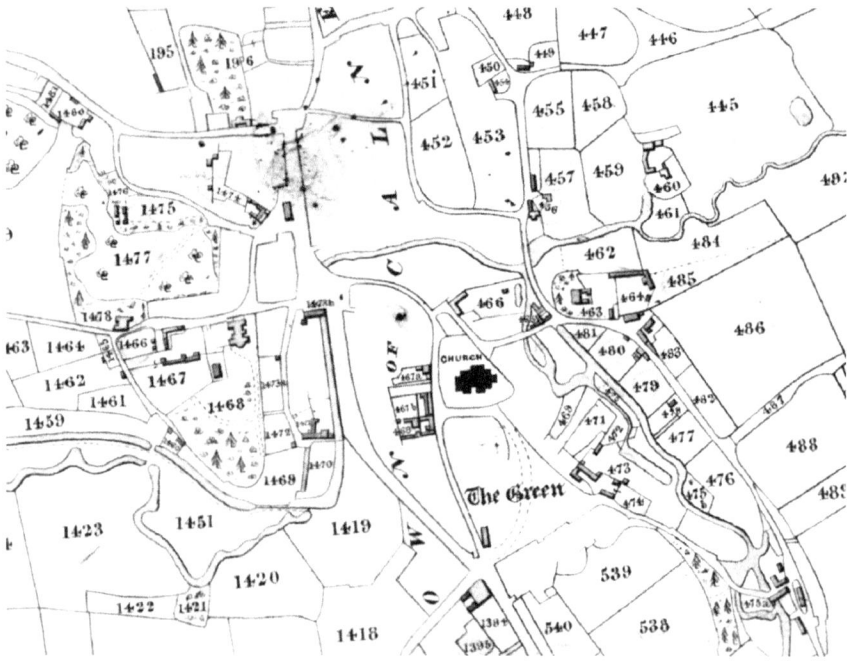

Figure 5: Calne in 1840 from the Tithe Map. Northfield House is at top 196. Many houses are omitted. "30 The Green" was just above the G in The Green.

A general practitioner of this time rarely had a large income. The surgeon doctor was dependant on having a caseload of local patients. In towns many of the patients came to the surgery, but in the countryside he often had to himself travel. Some would get a part time salaried position working for the local poor law board, but this was not well paid.

One way of supplementing a doctor's income was to take a single lunatic patient in as a supervised boarder. This could increase your surgeon's income by over 50%, did not need any payment for a lunacy licence and one could pay a servant to do most of the work. Make sure you had a quiet amenable chronic (female) patient and it was a relatively hassle free income boost.

Board more than one lunatic and you had to get an Asylum licence from the magistrates. Though one had to pay for the licensing, a private patient usually paid £1 - £5 a week at a time when a doctor's income was often only £2 – £5 a week. A lot of money could be made.

This time though was the heyday of private asylums – since Samuel Tuke had published his account of Moral Treatment at the quaker Retreat in York,[14] the message had been pushed that lunacy could be cured and that chains and beatings were not the method to use but understanding, minimal restraint and reward for expected appropriate behaviour. Asylums, or Madhouses, should not be feared nor should their 'Mad-doctors' who ran them. Workhouses were not the place for treating lunatics who could not follow workhouse rules, so after the 1834 Poor Law lunatics were expected to be treated in lunatic asylums. The private sector blossomed and fortunes were made as large numbers of pauper patients were corralled into the cellars and outhouses of private Asylums with little care. As an example, nearby Kingsdown House in Box was admitting paupers in large numbers and had over 100 pauper and 30 private patients at this time. We know they were charging private patients 25 shillings a week in 1814 and in the 1830s undercut the local prices for paupers at 8/- a week, making at least £4000 a year with costs probably under £1000. Though the mad-trade and profession of mad-doctor was not a popular one within the medical profession it could make people very wealthy and it attracted many mavericks as well as religiously inspired workers.

The level of care for pauper lunatics became a scandal and in 1845 the counties were forced to build county asylums for their pauper insane and the Commissioners in Lunacy were created as supervisors. They publicly abhorred the private trade in lunacy. As a result of the loss of pauper business and the Commissioners pushing for accommodation and treatment that was as good as that in the new County Asylums, most private lunatic asylums closed by 1860 – around Bristol and Bath, where up to seventeen private asylums are known, only four survived – Kingsdown House in Box, Bailbrook House in Bathampton, Brislington House, and Northwood House in Frampton Cotterell. These became mainly nursing homes for chronically ill genteel folk.

Lunacy Law is dominated by the fear of wrongful confinement of the sane person. The 1828 Madhouse Act required any proprietor who kept a single lunatic to obtain certificates as though they were confined in a licensed house (to stop the arbitrary incarceration of alleged lunatics). The notice of having a single lunatic had to be sent to London as a sealed private return, to authorities who changed over time, and fresh certificates sent every year. How far this was initially followed in practice is unclear but it was probably more universal by the time of the 1845 Lunacy Acts that created the central supervision of the Commissioners in Lunacy. The lunatic might be visited by an authorised physician, but the process was kept relatively private and covert until the 1890 Lunacy Act when all single lunatics had to be visited shortly after admission.

There was no provision for the voluntary admission of lunatics during this time, in part due to the great fear of wrongful confinement. In practice a person could be admitted as a voluntary resident either to stay with a doctor or to a licensed asylum but they were there as a lodger with the owner, no different to a physically ill patient or a paying boarder, but if it was discovered that they were indeed insane and were being confined uncertified then this was a serious offence with a hefty fine. Many of the patients staying alone with doctors were said to be 'nervous but sane' and were able to escape the awareness of officialdom unless someone complained. There was nothing in law to stop a mad-doctor taking sane patients as guests alongside certified patients, but the Commissioners in Lunacy who supervised the system hated any mix of voluntary and certified patients in a house as it was so open to abuse. After the 1853 amendment Act an ex-patient could stay as a 'boarder' but only if agreed by two Commissioners in Lunacy who had examined them, presumably to ensure the person was still compos mentis, able to agree to their treatment and were truly voluntary.

Figure 6: Northfield House, now called St Cecilia House

Northfield House then stood on the main road on the edge of Calne. It had the necessary benefit of a large rear garden. With modern developments it now is at the centre of the town renamed St Cecilia House, 6 The Square, providing accommodation for boarders at St Mary's School.

Northfield House was kept as a small Asylum for non-pauper genteel patients – only 25 certified admissions arrived in the 12 years between 30 May 1833 and 21 Jan 1845 with the busiest year being 4 admitted in 1839 (See Appendix for full list of patients). One woman was admitted twice, one three times. Of all 25 admissions 7 left cured, 8 left 'relieved' or 'recovered' – a 60% improvement rate, typical of the period (though study shows few lived independently afterwards). Five died and 5 left 'not cured' or their condition not stated. Most are from the neighbouring 20 miles but addresses further away include Poland, Westmoreland, Shrewsbury, Derby, Hereford, Kensington and two from Bristol.

The Asylum was visited regularly by the appointed local Magistrate Visitors who recorded their views in a local register.[15] Their reports are generally short and congratulatory but we do not have the patient book where they wrote more private views. The place developed slowly but grew as George gained confidence. The first patient, Miss Fussell, was transferred in May 1833 from Kingsdown House Asylum where she had been for 13 years. George said she could attend the family prayers which were read in the house but he found attending church made her worse. The Visitors note she had access to the extensive flower garden and books. She died after 4 years. After a year another woman was admitted who left 'cured' after 3 months. The following year 2 more women entered who both left much improved but were readmitted over the following years. The fifth woman admitted in November 1835 left cured within a fortnight. The first man admitted, in August 1836 was a surgeon who seems to have returned to practice.

George was only housing up to about three patients at a time, but clearly felt he could deal with more. The November 1838 visit notes that 'Considerable alterations and improvements are making in the House.' Unfortunately the building plans have not survived. The work was probably extending the west side of the house and adding a coach house along the road. In 1839 after completing the alterations, the Asylum expanded - 4 patients were immediately admitted and soon the asylum was generally accommodating 6 patients. In December 1839 there were 4 men and 2 women: 'The whole of the premises in excellent order and the Patients comfortable and healthy and properly taken care of. ... The [new patient's] rooms are large and well ventilated and the garden walks spacious and airy.'

Figure 7: Northfield House from the back has changed little today since the 1850s. The bedrooms built by George are probably the rooms on the right.

George was doing well financially by this time as in January 1839 he invested in 125 shares of the new British and Australian Bank and become a director, he sold the shares the following year for £2,500 (and so partially escaped later criticism of the bank and its workings).[16] He then invested in various Railway schemes that were blossoming around the area.

We know virtually nothing of the illnesses that his patients had. In this era many were physical such as third stage syphilis in men, though there is little evidence for this in his patients.

1841 Census: Calne Private Asylum [HO107/1168/5 f35]

George S Ogilvie	45	Surgeon Proprietor	No
Richard Gilpin	30	Patient – Gent	No
Richd Sisson	45	Patient – Gent	No
Richd Poole	20	Patient – Gent	No
John Beddoe	45	Patient – Merchant	No
James Fry	20	Servant	Yes
Mary Newton	45	Matron	No
Jane Tayler	30	Patient	Yes
Mary Palmer	35	Servant	Yes
Mary Smith	30	Servant	Yes
Mary Hanell	25	Servant	Yes
Curzon Street:			
James Pownall	30	Surgeon	No Jamaica
Lucretia Pownall	30		Yes
Isabella Pownall	20	Independent	No Jamaica
Robert Hill	20	Surgeon Asst.	No
Ann Blackman	20	Female Servant	Yes

The 1841 Census shows five patients including one woman. George was living in, with a paid matron, Mary Newton, and one male and three female servants to look after the house and patients. There may have also been some day-servants.

James Pownall is living nearby with his wife and sister, after recovering from his first illnesses.[17] Their mother in law, Bridget Bishop is also adjacent, probably in a small house next to the asylum. George's children are in boarding schools – the girls placed together in a girls' school in Cheltenham; son George in a school run in his rectory by the rector of Great Elm, near Frome.

When the magistrate visitors came in September 1842 Dr Ogilvie was away in Bristol bringing back 'Mr Sisson, a patient, on a visit to his Friends there and much better than he has been.' They met the other five patients and who 'appear to be in good health and evidently improved in regard to their mental state.'

The asylum peaked at seven patients on the December 1842 visit. Mr Beddoe [brother of the Bristol Iron manufacturer] appears 'free from any signs of insanity, but they understand that he is subject to paroxysms of despondency which in their opinion renders it desirable that he should remain under medical care.'

The idyll of Northfield changed with the arrival of the Commissioners in Lunacy. In 1842 the Metropolitan Commissioners of Lunacy who licenced the London Asylums were given authority to inspect all the asylums in the provinces that were licenced by the local magistrates. In 1844 they published a damning report on the poor care of lunatics when under the supervision of either the Poor Law Authorities or the local magistrates in the provinces. Their report rarely describes good practice, but it was a report with a purpose: it triggered the 1845 Lunacy Acts that compelled all counties to build their own pauper lunatic asylums and created the new Commissioners of Lunacy to be in charge of inspecting all Asylums in England, though in deference to the existing county magistrate visitors, local magistrates still had the duty of visiting and licensing the ones outside London, with the Commissioners visiting less frequently. This combination of parallel teams created a lot of potential conflict of opinion that had to be danced around, particularly as the local magistrates had a different set of priorities to those of the national Commissioners.

One preoccupation of the Commissioners was wrongful confinement. Whilst the magistrates clearly approved of Northfield House, the Commissioners' 1844 report focused on only one aspect of practice – having uncertified patients:[18]

> At our second visit, in 1843, to the house of Mr Ogilvie, at Calne, in the County of Wilts, we found that he was in the habit of receiving from time to time, a gentleman without certificates, who had been previously confined in his House as a Patient. This practice was objected to by us in the Visitor's book, and the Visiting Magistrates, on two subsequent occasions, expressed their entire concurrence in

our views upon this subject. At our fourth visit to this House, in April 1844, there were three persons, who it was said were not Insane, residing in the house as boarders. One of these persons was the gentleman who had been previously confined under certificates at Mr Ogilvie's [Mr Sisson], and another was a person who had been a certified Patient in two other Houses, and who, if not positively Insane, was in a very doubtful state of mind [Mr T C Hayward]. He had quarrelled with his own relations, who are highly respectable, and he expressed a desire to be reconciled to them. The person and property of this individual both seemed to be under the control of a solicitor, and we regretted that he was not under the care of the members of his own family.

Mr. Ogilvie advertises, that he receives Nervous as well as Insane Persons in his establishment.

… We have brought this subject before your Lordship's notice, in a special manner, because Boarders, represented to be of sound mind, have been removed from several Licensed Houses upon our suggestions, whilst at the Houses of Aspall Hall and at Calne, the practice of receiving them has been persisted in, notwithstanding our repeated remonstrances.

The names of the patients alluded to can be discovered from other sources. George does not seem to have admitted uncertified patients extensively as there are none in the 1841 Census.

The Commissioners do not say that the boarders are illegal but do not want the admission of uncertified 'boarders' to an asylum, though the magistrates seem to be more relaxed on the matter. Ironically almost ten years later the 1853 Lunacy Acts would allow boarders – for patients who had been previously certified but treated and discharged to return voluntarily and even for their relatives to join them. Ogilvie was anticipating matters but at the time in 1844 its legality was dubious.

The degree of freedom that Ogilvie probably gave his patients must have irritated the Commissioners as they later in the same report heavily criticised sending patients out freely in another asylum:[19]

> At the Gloucester Asylum, as has been stated to us, the Superintending Physician permits Patients, before they are discharged, to go home to their own families, and receives them again without requiring fresh Orders and Certificates; and ten or twelve Pauper Lunatics appear to have ingress and egress from the Asylum at all times, at their own discretion. This practice is contrary to law, and appears to us to be open to serious objections. …

The Commissioners were clear: It should be transparent at all times where a certified patient was and who was responsible for them. The Magistrate Visitors had made no mention of Boarders up to now in their official reports. At their next visit in August 1844 they allude to the Commissioners' report and note that Mr Sisson is still a certified patient whatever the Commissioners claimed, and:[20]

> With respect to the other parties alluded to it appears that a gentleman who has been a certified patient into different houses [T C Hayward] has been a boarder in this house for some considerable time and that there are two other persons in the house as boarders with Mr Ogilvie today. The visitors have on former occasions expressed opinions on the subjects in the patient's book [not copied elsewhere and now lost] and as there seems to be a difference of opinion upon the law thereon, the visitors submit the whole to the consideration of the court when Mr Ogilvie applies for a renewal of his license.'

The Magistrates were not going to be dictated to by London based Commissioners. George's licence was renewed as usual. In January 1845 the magistrates noted there were five certified inpatients, the boarders had all left 'apart from the gentleman to whom allusion has been repeatedly made'. At their last visit in May 1845 they were told that this boarder [Hayward] was now living in a cottage nearby and there were no boarders in the House.

Alongside their first report the Commissioners published a collation of the responses of all asylums to some statistical questions as to numbers admitted each year, discharges, deaths, but also ascribed causes of insanity and types of insanity. The return[21] for Northfield House (see Appendix 1) is useful as the numbers are so low that individuals can be identified. A final table of causes of death enables us to link the causes of death of four patients and so is included in their biographies.

The statistics show how the numbers increased from 3 – 5 patients to 8 – 9 with the new build. They also show that if you did not die, you left cured or relieved. Only one in 21 patients left not cured. In this period the definition of relieved covered the person being able to return home and take up some of their domestic or work duties. As such it was not a taxing criteria, especially as few of the patients admitted were violent.

Few people were admitted who were violent – the two admitted with Acute Mania or "raving madness" were two women in 1842 and 1843. The latter, Sarah Pickett, died after 10 days – her death notices says it was 'after 3 weeks distressing and painful illness.'[22] The two women admitted in 1842 were both eventually discharged cured. The men who were admitted had 'ordinary madness' where they were not violent but disordered in thought or conduct. Several of the men had alcohol as a cause of insanity. Men were said to be mad due to excessive study; women clearly do not study or are immune from such things - women suffered from religious anxiety. Many though are put down to hereditary causes.

There are two prominent absences to the types of insanity. Other asylums list cases of dementia and paralysis of the insane (end stage Syphilis, also called GPI) – Ogilvie lists none. So this was not seen as a place for old age dementia, or GPI. Given that GPI was a common cause of insanity and admission for male patients, it is unusual that George did not knowingly admit any. But GPI was a condition that started with confusion and ended with debilitation, conduct problems and seizures – possibly not the person for the ambience of the place. Given that Ogilvie was also boarding patients, he could not have many violent, noisy or 'dirty' patients.

The three cases put down to bodily disorder were all women and one must assume these were gynaecological or obstetric problems – neuraesthenia from anaemia due to heavy periods or even post-partum psychosis. In pauper asylums of this time many of the women admitted are clearly in states of malnutrition and severe poverty[23] and many must have improved from receiving a decent diet and rest. However Calne was a private asylum so should not have seen severe malnutrition except in cases of anorexia nervosa.

George closed the establishment as a registered asylum in 1845, when he moved to Bristol and took over Ridgeway House Asylum. Two patients were discharged on 23 Aug 1845. The final patient admitted, nineteen year old Jane Daubeny of Seend, left 'recovered' on 21 September 1845. The last certified patient in the asylum, George Sisson, who had generated such controversy, was removed as a certified patient on 23 September 1845 – he probably stayed though as a week later the Commissioners note a letter from Ogilvie 'stating that he had given up his license but would retain one gentleman as a single patient and some recovered patients as Boarders.' We know that Mr Hayward was one of the boarders who followed George to Bristol. One wonders if Jane Daubeny also became a 'boarder'.

One's impression is of an asylum for genteel 'nervous' patients, in a light and airy large house with a large garden. One or two patients are often out visiting or on a trip when the Magistrates visit. Mechanical restraint is only once recorded by the Magistrates (for a man in November 1840) and there is never concern about excessive control. It was a quiet and spacious house on the edge of a small rural town and must have generated a comfortable income for George.

References

1. Malew; St Marks; John Ogylvie of Arbroath and Catherine Corrin of Castletown married by licence 16 May 1787.
2. See baptisms and minutes of the yearly conference of Methodists.
3. Short obituary in the yearly conference page 420 – see https://books.google.co.uk/books?id=RygRAAAAIAAJ&printsec=frontcover&dq=editions:0bbUu-YN4LBfeUrg7Am&redir_esc=y#v=onepage&q=ogilvie&f=false accessed 30 April 2021.
4. Charles Atmore Ogilvie is described in the D.N.B. and Alumni Cantab. John is said to be of Whitehaven but died in Duloe Cornwall in 1839. No will can be found. John married Catherine Corrin on the Isle of Man in 1787 and a child Elizabeth Corrin Ogilvie was bapt in the Wesleyan chapel in Halifax. There are fellow preacher George Shadford in the yearly conferences. Charles Atmore was an Itinerant preacher in 1781 and in 1811 president of the Methodist Conference.
5. Salisbury & Winchester Journal 4 May 1818 p4d
6. Wiltshire& Swindon Heritage Centre Poor Rates 1815 – 21: G18/990/5
7. See his entry in the 1851 census
8. Manchester Courier 21 Dec 1850 p6.
9. Morning Herald 15 & 23 May 1850 p1. Also in Weekly Dispatch and Illustrated London News
10. In St Mary's school history of Northfield House/ St Cecilia's House and see entry for Rugby Union in South Africa in Wikipedia.
11. Crockford's Clerical Directory 1898 p1006.
12. Wilts Record Office G18/100/1 Minutes of Calne Borough
13. In the 1844 Metropolitan Commissioners in Lunacy report the date of opening is given as 14 May 1833.
14. Tuke, S. Description of The Retreat, an institution near York for Insane Persons of the Society of Friends. York, W Alexander, 1813. available online.
15. In the Wiltshire & Swindon Heritage Centre A1/560/2 along with the register.
16. See for example Sun (London) 8 Dec 1840 p4 for report of enquiry into operation of the bank and which lists George's holdings.
17. 1841 census – The Asylum is listed on a separate sheet so it is difficult to tell if they were the same site with different front doors. Robert Hill is not in later documents. But the name might be HIce or Alice – also not in other records.
18. The Report of the Metropolitan Commissioners in Lunacy to the Lord Chancellor. London: Bradbury and Evans 1844. Page 37 & 38
19. 1844 Report - Ibid. p166
20. Wiltshire and Swindon Heritage Centre A1/560/2 entry 9 Aug 1844.
21. Commissioners, L.. Statistical Appendix to the Report of the Metropolitan Commissioners in Lunacy to the Lord Chancellor. London.1844 p144.
22. Devizes and Wiltshire Gazette 11 Jan 1844 p 3 Death Notices
23. Unpublished analysis by Peter Carpenter of Leicester Asylum admissions 1845 – 55.

James' success in Calne

After qualifying in 1828 James first worked as a Surgeon Apothecary in Bath Street, Frome as he is stated to be there in 1830 and 1832.[1] However he then moved into partnership with his brother-in-law in Calne presumably as George expanded his practice by running Northfield House as an asylum. He becomes a voter in Calne in 1836 with a house on Curzon Street by Northfield House.[2] He first appears in records in practice there in 1837 when he gives evidence on the victim's injuries in a local murder trial.[3] He testified that the victims throat and blood vessels had been cut on one side by a sharp instrument – as he later also did.

At this time a surgeon would have had an office at home to see patients, but generally would have spent a lot of time travelling on horseback in all weathers to visit patients at home. You would have worked hard to develop a base of regular clients whilst following the etiquette of not actively poaching those of rival surgeons. Income was uncertain and many surgeons went bankrupt – joining a practice at least reduced the effort of starting up in a new place.

Pownall is reported to have had two early episodes of insanity in 1839 and in 1840. If the episodes were like his later ones he became stressed by overwork, then developed a fear that his food was poisoned, tried to kill himself and attacked others near him – possibly Lucretia or Isabella. There is a comment at his later trial that Pownall said he had pointed a gun at his wife, but merely to frighten her and this may refer to one of these episodes.[4] He had access to guns most of the time before his incarceration in 1859.

In 1839 he was admitted to Fishponds Asylum, under the experienced care of George Gwinnett Bompas, and then in 1840 to the newer purpose built Northwood House Asylum[5] under the effective care of Frances Hawke the female superintendent-housekeeper, with the medical proprietor Henry Fox visiting. His admissions or indispositions do not reach the print of newspapers. The later accounts all say that James fully recovered and he returned to Calne to continue with his medical practice in partnership with Ogilvie. But we know he soon returned to practice as he advertised in the newspaper in December 1840:

> CALNE:- the operation for the cure of squinting has been performed in very many cases, and in all with perfect success, by James Pownall, Esq., surgeon of Calne.
> *Bristol Mercury* 12 Dec 1840

He also gave evidence in 1841 as the attending surgeon on the suicide of a man by hanging.[6] In the 1841 census he is living on Curzon Street with Lucretia and Isabella, but more tellingly is not listed as living with George at Northfield House and Bridget, his mother-in-law is not living with him. James' house in Curzon Street gave him voting rights in Calne for the first time.[7]

These first episodes of insanity led to a cooling in the relationship between James and George. From later references it is likely that George arranged the certifications and admissions of James for Lucretia and both she and Isabella came to depend on his advice during this stressful time. If he tried to kill himself or threatened them this would have been very understandable. The Gloucestershire Chief Magistrate Purnell later wrote that James said he disliked the relationship that developed between George and his wife.

The relationship broke down - James' and George's business partnership was formally dissolved by mutual consent on 31 August 1841. Other working relationships also ended - James is cited as the local medical referee for the National Provident Institution with George as the Agent, from June 1841 to July 1842[8] though this had ended when they advertised in July 1842[9] that the business partnership had been dissolved. James certified a patient who was admitted to Northfield in 1843, he later certified a patient for George when he was operating Ridgeway House Asylum – for this to occur George and James were not allowed to be in partnership. However later patient movements suggest an informal relationship continued.

James had access to enough money to buy Northfield House and the medical business from George when George left for Bristol in 1845. Some of this may have come from the winding up of his father's estate in 1844. James' medical practice expanded and he appears to have been busy enough to engage an assistant: his 'surgeon's assistant' Robert Hill lives with him in the 1841 Census and his assistant Mr Springfield gives evidence in 1847. However neither assistant appears as a qualified doctor in later directories or registers suggesting they were not appointed as apprentices.

James was elected a town councillor for Calne in November 1844 as George Ogilvie retired from the Council. He attended few meetings and did not seek re-election after his standard three years.[10] He proposed the creation of and joined the public health committee in January 1849 but it is not clear how active he was there.

We have two public records of him being in conflict with others at Calne. In May 1847 he sued a horse dealer for selling him a defective horse. At trial he said he had once kept up to 6 horses at a time but now had only one. It is reported that he had previously sued another man for a defective horse and himself been sued for selling a defective horse to a Dr Everett. James' current assistant Mr Springfield gave evidence. James surprisingly lost his case despite witnesses confirming the facts.[11]

In September 1853, James pleaded guilty at the Calne court of assaulting a William Gibbs and was fined 1 shilling with 9d in costs. The court record is very abbreviated, with the usual witness statements not included. Who this William Gibbs was is not known. It is not reported in the local papers and seems to have been hushed up – but then it would have been embarrassing for the new chief magistrate to have a recent conviction for assault.

James Pownall, Mad-doctor

James Pownall bought Northfield House from George on 26th September 1845 just after the last certified patient left.[12] George departed to Bristol leaving him sole possession of the house, now able to accommodate seven or more 'guests'.

James continued as Surgeon Apothecary. He did not renew George's asylum licence for Northfield House but kept a single lunatic, which was allowed. In May 1847 he wrote to the Lunacy Commissioners reporting that his single patient Mr Pinniger had escaped and that 'parties' had assisted the escape and obstructed recapture.[13] Who this man was is not clear – but it is quite likely to have been Henry Crook Pinneger who was admitted to George Ogilvie's Ridgeway House Asylum on the 20 December 1846 and discharged recovered on 22 January 1847.[14] If so then there was still a working relationship between the two doctors. There were several prosperous Pinneger families in Calne in the 1840's – Henry Crook was born in Compton Bassett next to Calne, the son of farmer John Pinneger. He clearly recovered as he appears in Swansea in 1874 where he, a bachelor Grocer, marries a widow. He died in Swansea in 1877.

Pownall had seen George run foul of the Commissioners in Lunacy at Northfield House and watched from a distance the disaster Ogilvie had with the inspections of Ridgeway House Asylum. He proceeded to avoid a licence by admitting 'nervous people' as evidenced by this 1850 advert:

MENTAL AFFLICTION
NORTHFIELD HOUSE, CALNE, WILTS.
(Six miles from the Great Western Railway Station, Chippenham)
Mr POWNALL, SURGEON, continues to receive a limited number of MENTALLY-AFFLICTED and NERVOUS PATIENTS. The great advantages in this Establishments can be seen in a circular which will be forwarded (postage free) on application
Salisbury & Winchester Journal 29 June 1850

No copy of the circular has survived. In the 1851 Census he is living at Northfield House with his wife, 4 male and 1 female 'patients'[15] [without Pinneger] along with only a cook, groom and live in house servant – there are no attendants (See Appendix). The house is operating as a genteel boarding house for the mildly disordered with 'nervous' uncertified people. But calling the boarders 'patients' in the Census conveys an attitude that breached the law.

The Lunacy Commissioners got involved. In April 1851 Mr Joseph Phillips, of Calne wrote on behalf of the local magistrates to the Commissioners in Lunacy calling their attention to the fact of the reception of Insane Patients by Mr James Pownall – the Commissioners alerted one of the local Commissioner visitors.[16] However little seems to have occurred until one of Pownall's 'residents', farmer Samuel Chapman [listed in the 1851 Census] died at the end of June. Soon after this Mr Hitchcock the proprietor of nearby Fiddington House asylum wrote to the Commissioners calling attention to Pownall's house and the 'suicide' of Mr Chapman therein, though how he knew of it is unclear – it did not appear in the local newspapers so it must have been by local gossip. The Commissioners again referred matters to their local Visitor Mr Sotheron.[17] Sotheron responded and the Commissioners applied for the Lord Chancellor to order an inspection of Northfield House.[18] Pownall was inspected. The outcome was not in his favour as the Commissioners asked the Chancellor pay for a court case to be taken against James.[19] It was illegal to keep two lunatics or more for profit in a house without licencing it as an asylum. The fine could be £500, recognising the sums that could be made out of the mad-trade. The Chancellor took his time to respond but said that though Pownall had broken the law, there was no wish to prosecute provided he abstained from further admissions or obtained a licence.[20]

James obtained an asylum licence for Northfield in July 1852 for nine male and four female patients,[21] and proceeded over the next few days to certify the six residents. We do not know if anyone left when the place became an Asylum. He 'admitted' six certified patients between 9th and 12th July. He only admitted one other patient – on the 6 November 1853. They all have at least one of the medical certificates signed by a Calne doctor with the second certificate being based close by – in Bath, Chippenham or Melksham. Four of the first 6 certificates use Mr Langley the local doctor who later rented Northfield. They had not been certified in their place of origin before arriving so were all certified whilst living at Northfield.

The incident was reported in the next annual report of the Commissioners but they downplayed its seriousness – presumably as they did not want to lose face and appear toothless – they could only prosecute a person if the Treasury agreed to the expenditure and the Treasury was notoriously tight-fisted.[22]

> Since the date of our last Annual Report, several unlicensed houses, wherein persons represented to be insane were alleged to be illegally confined, … have been visited … In most of these cases, however, we found, after full inquiry, either that no legal offence had been committed, or that the violation of the law, even if it were capable of satisfactory proof, was, nevertheless, of so trifling and technical a kind, and was attended by so many circumstances of extenuation, grounded on the ignorance and poverty of the parties, and the total absence of *mala fides*, as to render the chance of convicting the offenders before a jury at best extremely doubtful. In such cases we have, in general, considered it advisable to abstain from resorting to legal proceedings, and have contented ourselves with taking effectual steps for securing a due observance of the law for the future.

The circumstances of the relicensing of Northfield House are not described in their report or in any reports of the quarter sessions. James avoided any fine for running an unlicensed asylum by getting it registered. His application to do this has not survived. He was required to demonstrate he was a suitable person to run an asylum though it was difficult for magistrates to refuse licences. It seems doubtful that he would have mentioned his own history of insanity in any licence application. Being a well respected surgeon in Calne was adequate recommendation.

Several of his patients came from non-conformist backgrounds (See Appendix 2). Two of his patients were discharged 'relieved' or 'improved' within a month of admission. One was discharged 'recovered' after 9 months. After the first week, only one new patient was admitted. None of those discharged before the closure of Northfield appear to have been readmitted to another asylum. The inmates who remained were all chronic patients who only left because the asylum closed.

As a licenced proprietor James Pownall submitted his views on Mechanical Restraint when requested by the Lunacy Commissioners and they are published in their 1854 Annual report.[23]

> As regards the treatment of the selected patients in my limited establishment, neither mechanical restraint or otherwise is resorted to.

James now was a successful man – he had a good income from his Asylum, with secure income from a group of chronic patients, combined with his more general surgical practice. Between June 1852 and November 1853 he acquired an M.D., probably by paying a fee rather than by study. We do not know which university granted the M.D.[24]

In November 1853, two months after he was convicted of assault, Dr. James Pownall (with his new M.D.) was re-elected Councillor, and immediately appointed Mayor and Chief Magistrate for the coming year.[25]

It is probably from this time that a photograph of him exists that has survived amongst his relatives. (See figure 8)

Figure 8: James Pownall in the 1850s from a family photograph.

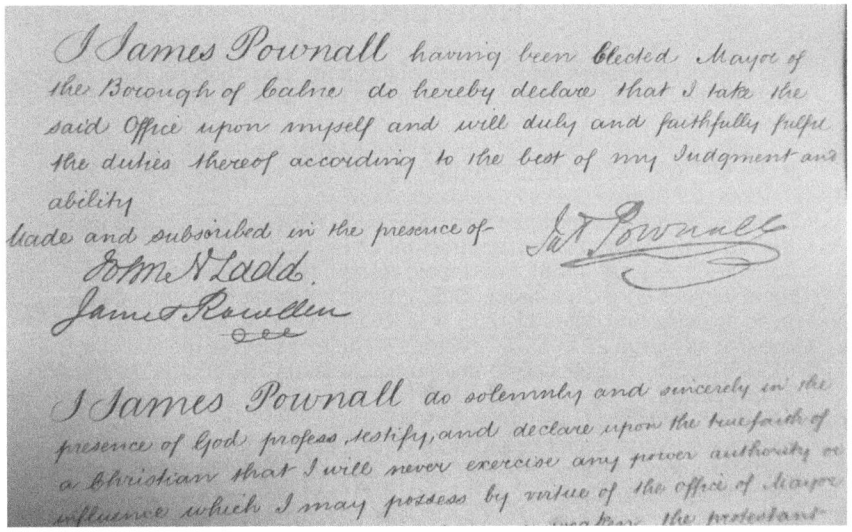

Figure 9: James signs his Oath of Office - from Minutes of the Borough of Calne

As Mayor he was expected to join another magistrate for the regular Calne magistrate court. However illness intervened at the end of March 1854: he only attended two council meetings as Mayor – that of January 1854 and 1st March. He stopped attending court as Magistrate in March 1854. The reasons for him failing to attend meetings are never mentioned in the minutes. He took no further public office after demitting as Mayor in November 1854.[26]

His only other public appearance in Calne in 1854 is in mid March when he gives evidence to the Coroner regarding attending a patient and finding severe cuts on the back of his head.[27]

References

1. See Pigots Directories for Somerset of this time. The 1856 court of chancery case states he was of Bath in 1830 but this may well be error or a private address.
2. Wiltshire & Swindon Heritage Centre: Borough of Calne Minutes and voter list for MP Nov 1836 G18/100/1 p52
3. Devizes & Wiltshire Gazette 16 March 1837.
4. Gloucestershire Chronicle 24 Dec 1859 p2d - this may possibly be a misrelating of the later very serious attempt on his mother in law.
5. Commissioners, L. (1860). Fourteenth Report of the Commissioners in Lunacy to the Lord Chancellor. (338.). London: House of Commons p92 gives asylums and dates of 1839 & 1840; Davey in his account says the first illness was at age 22 in 1829 (p49) but in the end talks of the first illness in 1839-40 (p56). The Gloucestershire magistrate lunacy records are missing for this period
6. Devizes & Wiltshire Gazette 5 Aug 1841
7. Wiltshire & Swindon Heritage Centre G18/100/1 Minutes of Calne Borough
8. Bristol Mercury: 19 June 1841; 16 April 1842; 25 June 1842; and Bristol Mirror 9 & 16 July 1842.
9. London Gazette 26 July 1842 p2057; The Sun 27 July 1842.
10. Wiltshire & Swindon Heritage Centre G18/100/1 Minutes of Calne Borough
11. Devizes & Wiltshire Gazette 6 May 1847 page 3
12. From short history of St Cecilia's House – sent by Mr A Harrison, employee of St Marys School. The house was sold as part of James' estate on his death.
13. National Archives MH50/2 minutes p150 15 May 1847.
14. National Archives MH94/ 07 Lunacy Admission registers patient 2699
15. National Archives: HO107/1837/folio 71 page 28
16. National Archives MH50/5 p11-12 Minute dated 10 April 1851
17. National Archives MH50/5 p89-90. Minute dated 17 July 1851.
18. National Archives MH50/5 p108 minute dated 31 July 1851
19. National Archives MH50/5 p169 minute dated 5 Nov 1851 and also p180 dated 8 Nov 1851
20. National Archives MH50/5 p263minute dated 4 Feb 1852
21. Salisbury & Winchester Journal 3 July 1852.
22. Commissioners, L. (1854). Eighth Report of the Commissioners in Lunacy to the Lord Chancellor. (339.). House of Commons – page 35 – 36.
23. 1854 8th report of Commissioners in Lunacy p205 – in same volume p9 note granting of licence. Ending is in 1855 report p1.
24. He says this in 1853 at the time of his election as mayor and in his will made 1859. The fact that he did not register it in the medical register is unusual and suggests it was not recognised in England as entitling one to practice as a physician. Some universities such as St Andrews would grant a Doctorate of Medicine (M.D.) to an established surgeon for £50 and good references. The source of the M.D. is never mentioned and cannot now be traced. It seems unlikely that James had the time to attend a university for over a year to get such a degree.
25. Devizes & Wiltshire Gazette 10 Nov 1853 Wiltshire & Swindon Heritage Centre G18/100/1 Minutes
26. Wiltshire & Swindon Heritage Centre G18/100/1 Minutes of Calne Borough
27. Wiltshire & Gloucestershire Standard 18 March 1854.

Ogilvie in Bristol:
Ridgeway House and its destruction.

Figure 10: Ridgeway House

George moved to Bristol in about September 1845 to take over the larger Ridgeway House Asylum after its previous proprietor, quaker Nathaniel Duck, died. He first appears to have planned to live and practice as a doctor more centrally in Bristol as when he applied for a licence on 12th September he said he would not be resident there and they might like to make his housekeeper the licensee (as at Northwood House Asylum). The magistrates said this could not occur so he responded on 12th October saying he would now reside at Ridgeway House.[1]

The initial contract appears to have been him renting the house and running the business on a short-term contract for Nathaniel Duck's widow. Many private lunatic asylums were in rented large private houses, as it saved the initial capital outlay. Proprietors might then sell on the asylum business to a new superintendent but keep a financial income from it.

In later testimony George states that he felt the building needed alterations but as he had only a short tenancy he postponed them. He also appears to have kept a second house nearby in Stapleton as later the patient Delafosse states he lived there with two other 'nervous' uncertified patients. This was probably where Hayward lived.

In taking over Ridgeway George also took over the care of Amelia Mais, James Pownall's cousin,[2] who had been there since 1832 and continued under his care. He also brought patients from Calne. He continued to care for Mr Hayward as a non-certified patient and took with him the certified patients Mr Richard Gilpin, Richard Poole and Jane Tayler. Mr Beddoe also re-entered his care after a year, suggesting his old contacts had some confidence in his practice. But Ridgeway House was a different enterprise to that at Calne – it was much larger than Northfield House and not so comfortably genteel - in January 1848 there were seventeen patients of which three were in restraint suggesting he was now dealing with a more disturbed population.[3] In addition he was dealing with the Magistrates of Gloucestershire who he did not know well. In April the Visitors comment that whilst Mr Beddoe is reported cured and is on a visit to Bristol, he should have been discharged formally before leaving even though he was planning to return. They also comment that Mr Pearce is under restraint and his detention defective as only one medical certificate was provided at the point of admission (though it was provided later).[4] In September Ogilvie reported that Beddoe was now discharged and Pearce was about to go on trial leave.[5]

George appears to have continued his practice of admitting 'nervous' patients as well as lunatics. In October 1846 he wrote to the Commissioners 'asking as to the right of relatives to confine an insane gentleman under special circumstances'.[6] An 'answer 'was 'directed' but we have no further details of the question or answer. It may have been about Delafosse but it suggests that Ogilvie was sailing close to the wind at times.

In 1849 things were well and George got a longer term lease so he started building a large modern extension to the place. But then disaster struck - the Chairman of the visiting Magistrates, Mr Purnell, started visiting and did not like what he found. What Purnell uncovered over the next six months at Ridgeway coloured his view of Ogilvie later, when George argued for James' continued detention in an asylum.

Figure 11: Mr Purnell Bransby Purnell Chief Magistrate of Gloucestershire

The Chair of the Gloucestershire Quarter Sessions and visiting magistrates, Mr Purnell Bransby Purnell, had started to examine the Gloucestershire private asylums in detail. In 1848 he made extensive complaints about the Fishponds Asylum. He held an enquiry and unusually published the proceedings.⁷ Whatever the merits, adverse publicity was the death knell for a private asylum. The licensee was changed but Fishponds Asylum never recovered and closed in 1859.

Purnell was concerned about illegal confinement and maltreatment. Confinement on illegal certificates was easier to prove and something he looked out for. There had been long standing concerns about wrongful detention of sane but inconvenient or wealthy relatives since the early 18th Century with Daniel Defoe and Smollet including it in their novels – this led to the 1774 Madhouses Act that required formal certificates to admit a patient to a madhouse. However anxieties grew as the private madhouse business boomed and Purnell made friends with the *Alleged Lunatic Friends Society,* who trumpeted the occurrence of illegal detention and poor treatment. Purnell became the scourge of private asylums in Gloucestershire.

At the March 1849 Quarter Sessions Purnell presented a series of cases of wrongful confinement at Fishponds. However he included one case from Ridgeway House - that of T C H [Hayward] – he read out a detailed description of the case that the papers immediately published. It read like a classic horror novel about wrongful incarceration, and played to public fears.⁸

Purnell's account was that TCH was a capable man. He had been the sole executor of his father's will, run two farms and then lived as a corn-dealer and maltster. As a single man, he made a will giving his estate to his brothers. In 1843 he became engaged despite his brothers trying to dissuade him. The next day he was taken to an Asylum by Salisbury on the order of his brothers. TCH says the reason given was his excessive use of alcohol which he put down to stress from arguments with his siblings. His keeper tried to stop him corresponding with his solicitor but he succeeded and by court order was examined by Dr James Cowles Prichard who declared him sane and he was released after seven months, £1200 the poorer.

The stress of these seven months and fear that his relatives would use any new excuse to declare him insane, made him depressed. He went to Mr Ogilvie's at Calne and lived there as *a nervous patient.* [and was the main person referred to by the Lunacy Commissioners in their complaint about uncertified patients at Northfield]. He moved with Mr Ogilvie to Ridgeway House, *continuing as a nervous patient; being however his own master, sleeping in lodgings, keeping his horse, and going and coming when and where he pleased.* However when he met and again was engaged to a highly respectable spinster, Mr Ogilvie seized him on the authority of his brothers, had him certified and confined in Ridgeway House. After nine months he managed to meet the magistrates despite obstruction by Ogilvie and his attendants, and was declared sane and discharged on 21st February 1849. TCH then discovered that whilst staying with Mr Ogilvie he had been tricked into signing deeds that prevented him from changing his will which gave everything to his brothers.

> [Mr Purnell reported that since TCH's discharge] an astonishing improvement has already taken place in his general health and appearance and [TCH] informed me of his having contracted marriage with the lady to whom he was attached. Subsequent letters show a continued improvement, the two last entered being in curious contrast; the one, an extract from Mr Ogilvie's, stating of him 'whom 99 persons out of 100 would unhesitatingly pronounce to be mad, as I believe would every competent medical authority;' the other from TCH ... giving me an account of his matrimonial tour, and stating, 'My health is now quite restored, with the exception of a slight cold,' and finishing – 'I am perfectly happy in the choice I have had the good fortune to make.' [9]

Mr Ogilvie responded at the magistrates' meeting by referring to supportive testimonials from Calne. He complained of the one-sided nature of the proceedings as he could not respond and give an account of TCH and asked for no publicity until he could do so. However despite his requests the report was fully reported in the press. Ridgeway House was publicly condemned as an asylum.

Ogilvie had written to the Commissioners about signing deeds: In November 1848 he wrote 're Henley': asking as to the legality of a Patient *'being made a party to proposed arrangement of partnership affairs.'* He was answered 'in the negative' which must have thrown later doubt on Hayward's deeds.[10] In Feb 1849 Ogilvie wrote a series of letters about Hayward to the Lunacy Commissioners, asking about the discharge and *'inquiring whether it was his duty to make and transmit to the Office copies of depositions and minutes entered by Mr Purnell and Dr Lyon in the Visitors Book relative to Mr Hayward's case'.* The Commissioners wrote to Purnell and Lyon asking whether depositions were intended as ordinary entries.[11] Ogilvie, in his role as superintendent, was required to send the Commissioners promptly a true copy of all entries made in the Visitors' Book. It clearly stuck in his craw to have to transcribe and send what Purnell and Lyons had placed there.

Ogilvie wrote to them again in early March to appeal about the magistrates' *'proceedings relative to the discharge of Mr Hayward'.* The Commissioners were not going to get involved. He was told he could not appeal to them but had to appeal to the Magistrates through their chairman or to the Home Secretary – he also had to make copies of the depositions and send them in as they were minutes of the examinations, but he was given extra time to do this.[12]

Things did not calm down – the next month the Magistrate visitors complained to the Commissioners that when they visited on the 18th April they found the Case Books defective. The Commissioners in turn asked them if this was 'of sufficient importance' to call for further proceedings?[13] Legal action is implied. No reply is noted.

Ogilvie then became embroiled with Purnell over his certification of another patient, Delafosse. George had earlier noted in April 1848 when there was a visit by the Magistrates (without Purnell) that *'Mr Delafosse still manifests his propensity to drink intoxicating liquors and is therefore, the previous history of his case being considered, unfit for liberation. He appears cheerful and contented.'* [14]

In Spring 1849 Purnell gave the required legal notice to Ogilvie that he was going to examine Delafosse regarding his insanity. Before the examination, George physically took Delafosse to the Lunacy Commissioners Offices in London unannounced and asked the Commissioners if a commissioner could examine him [as his insanity was being challenged]. The Commissioners were not going to get pushed into this and declined to examine Delafosse and dealt with Ogilvie's complaints about Purnell by again saying he had to take it up with the Justices or Home Secretary.[15] A few days later Ogilvie wrote complaining of Purnell's and Dr Lyon's examination of and discharge of Delafosse,[16] and the Commissioners invited Purnell to attend their next meeting for the 'interview he desired', but did not invite Ogilvie. Purnell attended and apologised for entries he had made about the visiting Commissioner – a dance of mutual respect occurred with Ogilvie blamed for any adverse entries but in the end the Commissioners still refused to get involved.

> Read further correspondence with Mr Ogilvie & his reply in explanation relative to a passage in his protest against Mr Delafosse's discharge and to which attention of Commissioners had been drawn by Mr Purnell.
>
> Mr Purnell attended the board by appointment, and explained the object with which he had desired an interview with some of the Commissioners. He stated his intention of bringing Mr Delafosse's case before the Justices in Quarter Session and charge Mr Ogilvie with a series of false Statements in his Books relative to Mr Delafosse's case, by which, Mr Purnell said, the visiting Commissioners and his colleagues, had been deceived. Mr Purnell with reference to some observations made by him in his last entry at Ridgeway House in illusion to the Commissioners, expressed his wish to disclaim any intention of reflecting upon them, and was assured by the Chairman that the Commissioners did not consider the remarks alluded to as at all offensive, or containing any imputation. Mr Purnell stated his wish to consult the Commissioners as to his

proper course of proceeding. The Chairman however informed him that the Board declined offering any advice upon the subject. Mr Purnell then retired.[17]

George Ogilvie then sent in a 25 page formal defence, dated 2 July, to the *'Lord Lieutenant and Magistrates ... as he had not been given notice of the report and so could not respond well in the meeting.'* [18]

> As an individual whose personal character and professional conduct has been traduced, and his pecuniary interest have been seriously prejudiced, by a Report made to you, by the County Chairman, and published by your Authority, I make to you an appeal, never made in vain to a Body of English Magistrates or English Gentleman, namely to hear patiently my answer to the charges brought against me, and having heard it, to do me justice.

His report directly and personally attacks Purnell. He argued that the asylum had been licensed for many years before him when it had many more patients. He took it over because its situation was excellent even if its accommodation had deficiencies. He did not carry out immediate improvements as he did not have a long tenure but when he obtained this in 1848 he had immediately set to improve the building by building a large extension. Purnell had first visited in 1848 and unexpectedly condemned the place, ignoring Ogilvie's planned improvements and the fact that he had not improved the old house previously as much as he was intending to do so now, and also ignoring the previously good comments by visiting magistrates and Commissioners about the house and its inmates - was Purnell saying the previous reports were wrong? As for the case of TCH – Purnell had been selective in quoting the evidence and changed some material to support his case, treating Ogilvie's opinions with *'supercilious contempt, to combat and misstate it, and afterwards to hold it up to public reprobation.'* Ogilvie cited that, because he had not been able to state who it was who told him of Hayward's threats of violence to a child at the time of certification, Purnell chose to believe Hayward's denials of any such threats. Moreover though he had the clerk interview the person threatened, that evidence was not cited. The evidence supported Ogilvie and that Purnell was not being impartial in his account. Ogilvie included as evidence the accounts of Sydney Smith and his wife who both said they knew Hayward well, he had lived with them and got on well with their child but he had in May become excitable and took a dislike to their child and threatened her so they were afraid to have him near them. They reported telling Purnell's Clerk of these threats. Similarly, Purnell said the Housekeeper reported Hayward had broken a blind but then that an attendant said he had himself broken it. He ignored the report by the Housekeeper that it was broken twice, once by Hayward and after repair again by the attendant. Purnell had insinuated that Hayward was never insane and always confined illegally but the visiting commissioners saw him as insane and the medical man his friends brought in to show he was sane said he was clearly insane.

He noted that the Chairman had said Ogilvie had improperly read a private letter from Purnell to Hayward. He pointed out that he gave the letter unopened to Hayward and after it was read, Hayward gave part of it to him to read and later showed the same letter to many people he happened to meet.

He added that Purnell was about to publish on another case [Delafosse] and asked it be delayed until they read the family's account of the case. He adds a defence of private asylums that anticipates his later arguments over the discharge of James Pownall.

> It is evident that the Chairman has become possessed of the idea that private asylums are public nuisances, that their proprietors are uniformly unprincipled and mercenary men, whose sole object is to get as many patients as possible and "cure being of course avoided" (as he says) to keep them as long they can find pretexts for preventing their liberation. The main objects of his Visits has consequently been to dismiss as many as possible, and to accomplish this, and thereby to do what he calls a great right – though, in reality,

it may be a great <u>injury</u> – <u>to the Patient</u>, he has not scrupled to do <u>great wrong</u> to the Proprietor. His idea is, that it is only dangerous Lunatics who require restraint and mental discipline; that "even though not sane, still patients who are neither violent to others nor to themselves and who labor only under harmless delusion, might by the intervention of their Friends be perhaps placed in quiet Lodging." Now this is an opinion that not only I, but much higher authorities than either the Chairman or myself believe to be most erroneous. …. The objects of such establishments are first, and chiefly the cure of patients, and secondly, their safe custody. This being, so there must necessarily be found in such establishments patients in various stages of disease and convalescence – some of them with periodical attacks and lucid intervals; other subject to irregular attacks of greater or less violence. In the milder stages of disease, and in lucid intervals patients are frequently so rational, and well conducted, that those unacquainted with the nature of the case would naturally be of opinion that they might be safely set at liberty, but this, experience has proved, would often prove dangerous to the public, and injurious to the patient. The discharge of patients under these circumstances, is one of the most anxious questions that can occupy the consideration of experienced Practitioners, and if <u>they</u> often err as undoubtedly they do in discharging patients, how much more likely to is a person who is not only unskilled in medical science, but who brings to the investigation an obstinate will and strong prejudices. …

I pray of [the magistrates] as a <u>man</u> whom the Chairman has <u>wilfully, most cruelly</u> and <u>most unjustly injured</u>, that I may be no longer subject to his insults and made the victim of his prejudices and consequent injustice.[19]

On the same day the solicitors also sent in their rebuttal. They had been accused by Purnell of misleading Hayward, and getting him to sign what he was told was a bond but which removed all his control of his estate. They called on the court to disown the allegations.

Hayward had approached them in 1845 to draft a trust deed to put his property into trust and protect it from his actions when insane without the cost and publicity of a Lunacy Enquiry. They had sought legal advice and it had been extensively discussed with Hayward over 3 months. Hayward had signed it willingly on the 21 November 1845 – his brother left the room so there was no charge of influence. The solicitors read through and discussed the content even though Hayward said it was unnecessary and wanted to sign immediately. He said he was not as well up on business as he used to be and wanted to obtain the assistance of the trustees. The legal opinion on the trust as set up was that when sane he still had the ability to control his property. [20]

The Quarter sessions commenced the next day. A newspaper report on them[21] says that Purnell was about to read a further report on his visits to Fishponds and Ridgeway House

> …when Mr Ogilvie, proprietor of the latter establishment, stepped forward and requested that a very long letter he had in his hand might be read before the Chairman read his report, as he wished to make a reply. He said he'd been very much grieved and misrepresented by the Chairman.'
>
> The Chairman said that at the last meeting, he (Mr Ogilvie) had had an opportunity of replying, of which he had not availed himself.

Purnell then read aloud his lengthy new report and seemingly ignored Ogilvie's. The newspaper reports on it suggests that Ogilvie's accusations of bias were well founded. He started with a comment about Fishponds and Ridgeway:

> The exposure of the last nine months of their management has proved that they require more frequent visiting and careful inquiry than the prisons of the country. Abuses which could not have occurred in prisons have been brought to light from the secluded departments of these asylums.

He updated them on the past cases:

> Mr TCH states that he is recovered in health, happy in his marriage, and trusts to be soon reinstated in his property. With reference to this, two physicians, one of the highest authority, have lately certified him to be of perfectly sound mind, notwithstanding Mr Ogilvie's averment that, if discharged, he might commit murder and suicide.

He then states that the lunacy law for paupers and for the rich is:

> Founded upon opposite principles, the [Lunacy] law for the poor on publicity, the law for the rich on secrecy and seclusion - they tend to produce the opposite results, of kindness and relief for the poor and of severity and retention for the rich.
>
> Still, publicity which is not injurious to the poor, would blast the future prospects of the young of richer classes....
>
> But this secrecy and seclusion is productive of serious abuses, principally arising from the profits of the proprietor being dependent on the retention of his patients.
>
> His interest is to obtain and retain the insane and the alleged insane - the curable and the incurable - and, maintaining their bodily health, to hurry them through the several gradations of mental disease, till imbecility ultimately accrues...

He made recommendations on how the laws of Lunacy could be changed.

He then turned to the case of Delafosse. Charles Walpole Delafosse was an old Etonian, and Oxford Graduate who later died in Jersey in 1860 at the age of 45.[22] The *Gloucester Journal* dedicated a full page to these proceedings but postponed the discussion of Delafosse's case to enable a further three columns the next week.[23] Purnell started by declaring:

> A gentleman has been confined under order and certificates during the last year and 3/4 as insane - there being no proof of his having been at any time of unsound mind...

> ...the several long and general accusations stated against the patient by Mr Ogilvie, in his case book, and which had evidently the effect of warping, from time to time, the sound conclusions which [past visiting Magistrates and Commissioners] had otherwise arrived at - they would long ere this, have given, as we now do to-day, notice of his discharge.

In July 1846 Delafosse 'of an amiable, but extremely facile disposition' had been sent in by his parents due to their worry about his intemperate habits. His certificate reported he had an utter lack of self control, and had attacks of excitement, and that only force stopped him from drinking. His parents later denied anyone said this.

> Mr Ogilvie placed him at a house in Stapleton, (not Ridgeway House), to live with two others, whom he called nervous patients, whom he allowed to drink a glass or two of beer daily at a public-house.

Delafosse had daytime liberty but a night-time curfew. He however went to a cricket match and stayed out one night and incurred a debt of 10/-. As a result his father was called and the young man agreed to stay at Ogilvie's for 12 months. During this he went to his parents for Christmas 1846 for a month. At the end of 12 months in April 1847 he had not been intoxicated but had incurred debts of 20/-. Ogilvie then wrote to his father saying he was utterly destitute of all moral principle and control, he was a case of moral insanity and should be confined legally as insane under a certificate. The father demurred but the son went to run away and Ogilvie then had his father sign a blank committal order which he completed later. Ogilvie appears to agree that this happened. The father seems to have signed it in case his son needed physical restraint.

The account is then that Delafosse absconded as he felt insulted by the housekeeper. He sold his jacket and travelled to Chippenham and then to Calne where:

He there borrowed a shilling of an old servant of Mr Ogilvie's, and took some coppers from the till[?] when opened by his daughter. These the old servant counted to be 8d, and got him a bed at Mr [Pownall], a surgeon. There he slept, and next day the 30th of July 1847, he breakfasted and dined, and was about to ride with that gentleman to Marlborough, when Mr Ogilvie and his head servant, with straitjacket and straps in a handkerchief, arrived, took him to Ridgeway House, without resistance, and locked him up there with the insane patients that evening.

How Delafosse knew people in Calne is never stated but one wonders if he had been a boarder there under Ogilvie. Purnell relates that James Pownall signed the medical certificate though he was related to Ogilvie and was once his business partner, and ran a house for nervous patients. Delafosse's confinement in Ridgeway with insane patients occurred the evening before his committal papers are dated. A Mr Mayor[24] completed the second certificate two days later stating his extreme addiction to intoxication made him insane yet the principal servant declared he had never seen Delafosse severely intoxicated. Purnell then argued that Ogilvie grossly exaggerated his level of drinking and wrongly said he was a liar and *'would scruple at nothing to obtain liquor.'* Delafosse denied any of the examples given and had witnesses for many of them. Purnell publicly charged *Mr Ogilvie with being morally, if not legally, guilty of forgery in the preparation of* the certificates.[25]

The newspaper reports also state that a relative of Ogilvie signed the committal certificate without having met Delafosse. Ogilvie was obviously a man who schemed to wrongfully admit patients. However the reports show that James Pownall signed the first certificate after he met Delafosse at Northfield House. Mr Mayor signed the second certificate[26] but was not related and was close enough to have visited.

A few magistrates then refuted parts of Purnell's allegations about some of the patients he discussed – the description of patients was not as they had observed, and others wondered if the public venue of the Quarter Sessions was the appropriate place to discuss such matters. They then read the letter from Hayward's solicitors, which the newspapers printed in full including the allegation that Purnell had met their response with *evasive replies*. In the meeting Purnell responded that four opinions had been taken and he still held that Mr Hayward was unlikely to have understood it and did not behave later as though he had. The magistrates then passed a resolution that there was no foundation to the imputations about the solicitors. They were not going to risk a legal battle with them.

Ogilvie's letter is then noted by the newspapers to make very serious imputations on the character of Purnell. The magistrates closed ranks and were not sympathetic to Ogilvie. They agreed to print Purnell's second report on Ridgeway House and said that the accusations against Ogilvie were serious and that they ought to pause before granting any licence renewal. They would not appoint a committee of investigation as Ogilvie asked as this would effectively put Purnell on trial. Purnell himself said all he had done was quote what Ogilvie had said then pointed out the inconsistencies.

The affair feels like open warfare. In their next visit to Ridgeway at the end of July 1849 eight of the Magistrates visited instead of the usual two. They complained about the care of Amelia Mais who wet the bed every night; where she was kept and the straps used at times. Ogilvie responded that Mais was a lot better than when he first took over her care, She was in a single bedroom as it was impossible to keep her near other bedrooms (due to the smell) and was near her attendant. He had altered the bed's arrangement, but she still wet her bed. As the visitors complained about the room, he had felt forced to move her to another room, that was the workshop of Mr Hayward before he was discharged, but the Visitors were still complaining. The Visitors also wrote to the Commissioners saying the Commissioners had not been shown her room when they last visited.

At the next Quarter Sessions, Purnell noted that[27]

> Mr Ogilvie had, in his published replies to the reports, denied the correctness of its facts, and alleged that circumstances had been perverted and exaggerated. In consequence of this, he (the Chairman) had called upon Mr Ogilvie to point out in what particulars the facts had been exaggerated; but although he had had several interviews with him, with that object, he had failed in obtaining any explanation from Mr Ogilvie. The Chairman went on to state that in his first notice of application for renewal of his license, Mr Ogilvie made it on his own behalf, as surgeon; but subsequently, at the suggestion of the committee of visitors, had expressed his intention of [applying as a gentleman and not as a surgeon and] having a medical gentleman appointed with him, to be appointed by the Court. He was requested to nominate a medical gentleman, …. That morning he had nominated Dr George Rogers …of whom the court could not fully approve, being himself the keeper of an asylum. … [then] Mr Ogilvie announced that having made arrangements which would dispense with the necessity of an application for a license, he begged to withdraw his notice of such an application.

Ridgeway House officially closed as an asylum – presumably just as the expensive building works were completing. As part of his aborted renewal application in October 1849 Ogilvie sent in a list of his current 12 patients. The Asylum closed as a Licenced asylum in mid November 1849 as on the 15 & 16 November 1849 four patients (including Amelia Mais) moved to Longwoods House in Long Ashton, operated by George Rogers. Three more moved at the same time to other asylums - one each to Brislington, Gloucester and Fiddington House. Patient Wansborough went to Northfield House as an uncertified patient/boarder.

Ogilvie retained four patients who were declared as 'visitors' with the family in the 1851 Census: Rachel Hardy, Diana Stokes; Frederick Hulme (who died in 1851) and Richard Poole. Richard had been admitted a patient at Northfield House in October 1839, and stayed with George until George died. Poole then lived as a single patient with another doctor in Portishead until he died. The 1851 Census has a fifth visitor from Calne, Mary Viveash, but she may have been a friend – she is recorded in the later censuses as living with her parents.

So George kept Ridgeway as an unlicensed asylum, receiving one single patient and a few 'voluntary Boarders'. A year later during the January 1851 Assizes the Clerk of the magistrates wrote to the Commissioners alleging Mr Ogilvie was illegally receiving insane patients at Ridgeway House. The Commissioners looked at arranging a visit.[28] Ogilvie was clearly keeping a single patient and other voluntary patients as he then asked if he could keep a second single patient in a cottage in the grounds. He was told not if it was also occupied by him [and legally part of the same property].[29] Gaskell and Campbell then visited and reported back to the Commissioners.[30]

George Ogilvie then looked at moving to London out of the way of Purnell – in June he applied to the Commissioners for a licence to operate Blythe House, near Turnham Green for 8 – 10 gentlemen and 3 – 4 Ladies.[31] This was a new venture as it was not currently licensed but it was in London where the Lunacy Commission was sole regulator. The Commissioners responded that given their frequent remonstration with him over receiving Insane persons as Boarders in evasion of the Act and the past report [of Gaskell's] they were not prepared to entertain the application.[32]

What is surprising is that Ogilvie looked to London and not another county such as Cornwall or Lancashire where the local Magistrates were not closely linked to Purnell and knew little about the case. Perhaps he felt the published newspaper reports were so bad that his best chance was with the Commissioners.

A few days later a representative of the Lord Chancellor advised the Commissioners that Ogilvie had in his opinion violated the Lunacy

Act, but as the report [of Gaskell] did not allege that he had in anyway mistreated any of the patients the Chancellor would not prosecute. The Commissioners could make up their own mind about the licence – they wrote telling Ogilvie to *'forthwith take steps to relieve himself from his present liability to prosecution.'* [33] He responded asking what steps were these? (and what about that Licence?) He was advised to discharge those patients received without legal authority.[34]

Ogilvie said he would get all his patients certified and placed out separately as single patients, but were they prepared to give him a licence? He was told by the Secretary that *'he was not instructed to give any assurance'.*[35]

Finally Ogilvie sent in a collection of opinions by medical practitioners declining to certify any one of his four patients as proper to be confined. He was told that if they were *'of sound mind and free as to property and person, law not violated.'* [36] He was told to resubmit a licence application but this did not happen.

Ridgeway closed to patients and the building was sold on in 1853 and eventually became a school.[37] George stayed in Bristol. There is a brief mention in the early 1850s that he is of Redland Green, and the contents of his house at Redland Green are sold at his death, but all the censuses and later directories show he moved to Merrywood Hall,[38] now the site of Southville Primary School. Here he was in Somerset and out of the remit of the Gloucestershire magistrates.

In 1853 he registered a patent for improved design for candlesticks and lamps.[39]

Purnell had ruined the reputation of Ogilvie's asylum. Ogilvie had accused him of hating the private asylum business and Purnell explained why, saying that a trade in lunacy encouraged wrongful detention. The clash had been over whether his patients were insane or not and when they must be released. The arguments would be repeated in a decade's time.

Purnell's arguments and criticism of Ogilvie are detailed. They accuse him of blatantly giving the worst interpretation of people's actions to further his profits. They paint him as a liar, cheat and non-gentleman. The Commissioners saw him as a troublemaker. Yet he was well regarded in Calne, and had voluntary patients when the officials only wanted certified ones. He can be seen as a champion of patients or as a grasping abuser of the vulnerable. We can all form our own judgement.

References

1. Letters in Gloucester Archives Q/AL/40/27
2. See Gloucester Archives: Q/AL/40/25 – the list of patients in 1843. Ogilvie is writing from Ridgeway in October 1845.
3. Gloucester Archives Q/AL/40/29 copy of CoL Report on visit 22 January 1848,
4. Gloucester Archives Q/AL/40/29 copy of Visitors report [not including Purnell] on 25 April 1848
5. Gloucester Archives Q/AL/40/29 note by Ogilvie dated 6 Sept 1848.
6. National Archives MH50/1 p382.
7. Gloucestershire Quarter Sessions. The Evidence Taken on the Inquiry into the Management of the Fishponds Private Lunatic Asylum. G. Q. Sessions. Bristol, Joseph Leech. 1848.
8. See for example Bristol Mercury 24 March 1849 where quotes and most of the information derives.
9. Bristol Mercury 24 March 1849
10. National Archives MH50/3 minutes of Commissioners in Lunacy page 233 dated 30 Nov 1848
11. National Archives MH50/3 minutes of Commissioners in Lunacy page 338 dated 19 Feb 1849.
12. National Archives MH50/3 Minutes page 355 2 March 1849
13. National Archives MH50/3 minutes of Commissioners in Lunacy page 404 dated 26 April 1849.
14. Gloucester Archives Q/AL/40/29 note by Ogilvie dated 6 Sept 1848.
15. National Archives MH50/3 p418 10 May 1849.
16. National Archives MH50/3 minutes of Commissioners in Lunacy page 428 dated 17 May 1849
17. National Archives MH50/3 minutes of Commissioners in Lunacy page 444 dated 8 June 1849.
18. Copy in Gloucester Archives Q/AL/40/31
19. Copy in Gloucester Archives Q/AL/40/31
20. Copy in Gloucester Archives Q/AL/40/31
21. Extracts from Bristol Times 7 July 1849 p3 and also from Gloucester Journal 7 July 1849 p4 'Trinity Sessions'

22. See national admission lunacy register, and his probate for 1860 plus entries in alumni Oxoniensis etc.
23. Gloucester Journal 14 July 1849 p4 'The County Chairman's third report on Lunatic Asylums.'
24. Presumably Emilius Scipio Mayor surgeon for the Lawson Gate house of correction Bristol Times 7 July 1849 p3
25. Bristol Times 7 July 1849 p3 Emphasis in original
26. Gloucester Archives Q/AL/40/31 copy of report dated 18 may 1849.
27. Bristol Mercury 20 October 1849 p4c Private lunatic asylums and see also Gloucester Archives Q/AL/40/31 correspondence for 1849
28. National Archives MH50/4 p405 dated 9 Jan 1851
29. National Archives MH50/4 p472 , 20 March 1851
30. National Archives MH50/5 p2 dated 3 April 1851
31. National Archives MH50/5 p61 dated 12 June 1851.
32. National Archives MH50/5 p145 dated 3 Sept 1851
33. National Archives MH50/5/p74 dated 27 June 1851.
34. National Archives MH50/5 p85-6 dated 10 July 1851
35. National Archives MH50/5 p92 dated 17 July 1851
36. National Archives MH50/5 p145 dated 3 Sept 1851
37. Bristol Archives draft deed 37918/D/20/42 for Ridgeway house dated 1856
38. See 1851 and 1861 Census
39. Patent no 688 registered 9 Nov 1853 – see London Gazette 4 Apr 1856 p1257

James' 1854 Bout of Insanity

James' first well documented episode of insanity occurred in 1854 under the stress of his new mayoralty and work as chief magistrate. In 1859 after another episode James' wife described this 1854 episode and its background to the Commissioners:[1]

Wroughton 23 May [1859]

I have been married nearly 32 years during which time my dear husband has had three or four attacks of insanity but the two last have been by far the most fearful. In the year 1853 he was in general practice at Calne in Wiltshire and we had an establishment for insane patients, that year he was elected Mayor of Calne, he had a great many things to attend to and constantly day and night work which I am sure was more than he could bear. In 1854 he got into a low depressed state, looked very ill complained of pains in his feet, legs, &c.

I should remark here that his Father was a Martyr to Gout and before my poor husband's attacks he has always something like suppressed Gout, once or twice he has had a little inflammation in his toe which relieved him wonderfully, but it is never of long continuance but gone in a day and night and then all the distressing symptoms return.

He then complains sadly of indigestion, heat in his stomach &c and from being most active and energetic he seems to lose all energy and becomes dreadfully depressed and cannot sleep well at night. The said sensations in the stomach continuing he then fancies something of a poisonous nature is given him, look suspiciously at all he eats carefully wiping his Plate, Glass &c and generally fixes on someone residing with him as the poisoner. He looks upon the person with sorrow and dread depicted on his countenance and the malady daily increasing the suspicion becomes more decided and violence to the person suspected is the result. This feeling caused him to strike a gentleman residing with us. Always with these attacks he attempts suicide.

He is naturally extremely kind and generous and when sufficiently recovered to know he has or attempted to injure a person he is most sorry and distressed and often exclaims "What have I done", "What could have induced me" &c.

The Commissioners first knew of problems in May 1854 when they received the following letter:[2]

Calne Vicarage, Wilts.

My Lord and Gentlemen

I beg leave to acquaint you with the following circumstances which have taken place at the Lunatic Asylum of Dr Pownall in this town of which I am one of the Visitors.

On Sunday Morning April 30 as Captn Warren and myself came out of the Church, a Police Officer accosted us, and said that one of the inmates of Dr Pownall's Establishment (Mr Tonge [Tongue] by name) appealed to us for protection - he was at that time at the Police Station. On going up to see him we found that he had sustained no bodily injury of any consequence but was in a great state of terror and alarm - Mr Pownall having in a moment of excitement and exasperation struck him.

I went up to see Dr Pownall, whom I found in a grievous state of depression and sorrow, after the momentary excitement was over, and no longer in a fit state to take proper charge of Lunatic patients.

Mr Ogilvie, who formerly had charge of the House, was then sent for from Bristol – he arrived in the evening and took charge (*pro tem*) of the establishment. Mr Tonge had been persuaded by me to return quietly to the establishment some hours before, and the evening and night passed in uninterrupted quiet.

I should say that Dr Pownall had been for sometime overworked in mind and body for some few weeks past, and had exhibited some days before such symptoms of nervous irritability, that a change of scene and the rest had been represented as absolutely necessary, but he had returned too soon and the unfortunate occurrence took place which I think it my duty to describe.

Dr Pownall went away with Mr Ogilvie yesterday to Bristol and some competent person is expected to arrive tomorrow to take charge of the Patients, his usual assistant is in the House and Mr Tonge's friends have been written to as his case is one which requires attention in the first instance.

I think it my duty also to state that this was not the first time that Mr Tonge had been assaulted by Dr Pownall, but that the same melancholy fact had recurred once before about a fortnight back previous to Dr Pownall quitting home as above related. All this was unknown to me, until a day or two ago. The general kindness exhibited by Dr Pownall to his Patients, when in his sound state of mind is a proof that he must be labouring under a nervous irritability, which rendered him for the time unfit to discharge the duties of his position. ….

John Guthrie [Vicar]

The letter does not mention any suicide attempt by James. So James' two assaults on Tongue, probably with a poker, was hushed up and he was sent for a rest, probably with his sisters in Bristol for over a week before he was admitted to Munster House Asylum in Fulham [opposite modern Fulham Post Office] on 11th May 1854, as 'dangerous to others'. His victim, the artist Richard Tongue, was in his absence transferred to Kingsdown House in Box on 26 May 1854[3] and the Commissioners had the licence temporarily transferred, presumably to Ogilvie.[4]

Munster House in Fulham was run by Cyrus Alexander Elliott and held thirty-five private male patients.[5] Cyrus was a surgeon who was experienced in Lunacy - he had operated Lunatic asylums since at least 1841 and rented and ran Munster House as a male only asylum for the 'Nervous, Epileptic and Insane' though we have no record of him taking uncertified patients.

James left Munster House 'cured' on 3rd June[6] and returned to run his asylum. Three weeks later on the 23rd June, an inquest heard that the previous day James was strolling in the garden with a loaded shotgun to shoot blackbirds attacking his fruit trees when he accidentally shot one of his patients: 37 year old Lieut. Samuel Arden who was helping by scaring out the birds.[7]

> I went towards my garden adjoining Northfield House, with a double barrel gun which was loaded with shot in one barrel only, for the purpose of killing blackbirds: they have been destroying the currants. In five or ten minutes after I have been walking between the garden and the lawn, whilst deceased was walking up and down throwing stones for the purpose of driving any birds out of the bushes, it's so happened that as I was carrying the gun in my hand, one of the barrels, which was only loaded, suddenly was discharged, and the deceased coming towards me at the time, within a few yards of the spot, received the contents of the gun into his left leg four or five inches above the ankle. I called for assistance and the deceased was immediately brought indoors.[8]

One of the Surgeons called, Mr Langley, gave the following additional evidence:

> I found the deceased upstairs lying on the bed. Both bones of his left leg were fractured – apparently from a gunshot wound. The muscles and soft parts were severely lacerated and there was a little bleeding. He appeared very weak and exhausted. The usual remedies were applied and Dr Pownall sent off to Bath to Mr Church, Surgeon, requesting him to bring a Hospital Surgeon with him. [they arrived and] … after waiting a little while and examining the leg, the surgeons came to the conclusion that the leg must be amputated which was soon afterwards performed by Mr Norman…. Deceased bore the operation very well. No chloroform was administered and there was very inconsiderable loss of blood during the operation. I left the deceased about 10:30 o'clock last night under the care of Mr

Church, who remained with him till he died about 5 o'clock this morning. Mr Samuel Arden told me that he was frightening the birds out of the bushes for the doctor to shoot them when the gun went off.

The cause of death was from the combined effect of the injuries to the leg of the deceased and the shock to the system from the operation.[9]

James was not asked to explain why he had loaded only one barrel when planning to shoot many birds. The verdict of the inquest jury was Accidental Death. James deteriorated after attending the inquest. He probably tried to kill himself and was immediately readmitted to Munster House under Mr Elliott on 26th June labelled 'suicidal and dangerous to others'.[10] Again there is no mention of his illness in the local papers other than his evidence as attending surgeon being read at an unrelated inquest 'the Doctor, unfortunately being unable to attend from indisposition'.[11] Having a mad Mayor, magistrate and town surgeon was seen as private and personal.

The Commissioners noted the death from gunfire in their meeting of 29 June when they:[12]

> Received notice, signed by Dr Pownall, and a statement of particulars in his absence, from Mrs Pownall. Death caused, as alleged, by Dr Pownall's gun, having gone off accidentally. Verdict accordingly. Letters directed to the friends of Mr Besant and Mr Wansbrough, the two remaining patients, urging their immediate removal to other establishments. These letters were directed partially in consequence of a communication, verbally made to the Secretary by Mr Heneage, MP for Devizes, to the effect that Dr Powell had left Northfield House under charge of a Keeper, and that there was a reason to doubt the propriety of the verdict.

The patients were all transferred to other asylums between 6th and 12th July 1854 exactly two years after their original certification. Northfield House Asylum closed and apart from the ending of the licence the Commissioners fail to mention the events in their annual report of 1854 or 1855.

The house was rented out, ironically to the surgeon who had attended Samuel Arden, William Langley (who also later became mayor of Calne). [13]

The family seem to have been unhappy with James' treatment with Mr Elliott, as after a fortnight he was transferred to the care of the more famous Forbes Benignus Winslow. Forbes Winslow was a surgeon who had developed a great reputation as a Psychiatrist, after writing books such as *The Anatomy of Suicide*, *The Plea of insanity in Criminal Cases* and *The Incubation of Insanity*. In 1848 he founded the Journal of Psychological Medicine and was a rejuvenating force in the *Association of Medical Officers of Asylums and Hospitals for the Insane* (the forerunner of the Royal College of Psychiatrists). He was a well known and well regarded psychiatrist. His son was later called in on the *Jack the Ripper* case.

Figure 12: Modern image of Sussex House, by the Thames

James was transferred 'relieved' on 11 July 1854 from Munster House to Sussex House Asylum, Hammersmith overlooking the Thames. The move did not go smoothly as on the 13th July Mr Elliott and Dr Winslow jointly attended the Commissioners as Winslow complained Elliott had obstructed the transfer. The Commissioners held a mini-enquiry and decided 'Mr Elliot's explanation sufficient'.[14] Then Winslow complained that one of the medical certificates admitting James to Munster House was signed by a Dr Bascome who falsely claimed he had an Edinburgh degree.[15] The Commissioners carried out a protracted correspondence and admonished Bascome [who in the Medical Directory the next year claimed an MD from Erlangen)

James Pownall was discharged from Sussex House after 3 months on 24 October 'not improved'.[16] This indicates that Winslow felt he was still a risk. He was sent to 'apartments near London',[17] presumably as a single boarder or a 'nervous patient' supervised by a surgeon. After more than twelve months he joined his wife who now lived in the village of Wroughton by Swindon, a quiet village a few miles from Swindon and its railway, with several farms and country residences. He lived there[18] ...

> for nearly three years, my poor husband being generally in excellent health and spirit and greatly beloved by all around him. He has taken since we have resided here an immense amount of exercise, hunting three or four times a week and walking a great deal during the shooting season but he tires more from walking than from hard horse exercise.

James was not struck off as a doctor but it was not possible to do so at that time - the current licensing and registration of doctors to practice did not exist. He may have had a small medical business at Wroughton, looking after his family and friends, but mainly lived the life of a gentleman, living off the rent of Northfield House, and presumably the income from his father's bequest and Lucretia's assets though the cost of his recent spell in care must have drained the coffers. His mother-in-law still lived with him and had her own income as did his sister Isabella Pownall. He stopped being listed as a house owner in Calne in the October 1855 voter list.[19]

Lucretia's account of his hunting and shooting and being well liked in the area rings true. In 1855 he was prosecuted for trespassing when shooting game. In 1856 he was the man who proposed *'the health of the bride and bridegroom ... in a very feeling and appropriate speech'* when the village celebrated the return of local squire Philip Pavy of Elcomb Hall from his honeymoon.[20] In his will he later left gifts to five friends in Wroughton including £100 to Fanny Pavy the daughter of Mary Pavy of Elcomb Hall ... *'as a small acknowledgement of the kindness I received for three years.'* [21]

References

1. In Gloucester Archives: Q/AL/46 page 5ff. Copy of letter
2. In Gloucester Archives: Q/AL/46 page 17. Copy of letter
3. From the Lunacy registers [Nat Archives MH94p09] Richard was [re]admitted Northfield house 12 July 1852 and discharged 26 May 1854. The Kingsdown register WSHC A1/560/1 has him admitted the same day as patient.
4. Nat Archives MH50/7 p53 minute dated 25 May 1854
5. Eighth Report of the Commissioners in Lunacy to the Lord Chancellor. (339.). House of Commons 1854
6. Lunacy registers [Nat Archives MH94p09] patient 7232
7. Wiltshire Independent 29 June 1854 has longest account of inquest.
8. In Gloucester Archives: Q/AL/46 page 22f. Copy of statement of James Pownall at Inquest.
9. In Gloucester Archives: Q/AL/46 page 25f. Copy of statement of Mr Langley.
10. 1860 Commissioners Report p93
11. Devizes & Wiltshire Gazette 10 Aug 1854
12. Nat Archives: MH50/7 p87
13. See 1861 and 1871 Census and the sale particulars of the newer part in Wiltshire & Gloucestershire Standard 17 July 1883.
14. Nat Archives: MH50/7 p108 dated 13 July 1854.
15. Nat Archives: MH50/7 p121 dated 26 July 1854 also pages 132;142;145; 157 and 175.
16. Lunacy registers [Nat Archives MH94p09] patient 7447 & 7515
17. See wife's account in Gloucester Archives: Q/AL/46 page 5ff.
18. In Gloucester Archives: Q/AL/46 page 5ff.
19. Wiltshire Swindon Heritage Centre: Borough of Calne Minutes and voter list G18/100/1 for 9th Oct 1855.
20. Wiltshire & Gloucestershire Standard 16 August 1856.
21. Will central probate registry James Pownall MD 1883.

James' 1859 bout of insanity

In 1856 James was sued in the infamous Court of Chancery.[1] His sister Mary Ann Britton and her five children jointly sued the three trustees of her father's bequest to her, namely:

- Jeremiah Mais who was an early son of Charles Mais by the 'free quadroon' Ann Ivey in Jamaica. Jeremiah married Charles' stepdaughter and Mary Britton's cousin, Emmeline Bennett. He was a customs and excise officer.

- John Mais, clerk of Tintern Parva, also a son of Charles Mais by Ann Ivey.

- Her brother James Pownall 'of Calne'

The case was that when Mary Ann married in 1832 a marriage contract was executed moving her portion of the estate of her father James Corne Pownall into a trust for her use (independent of her husband) and then after her death to be given to her surviving children or used as she directed. The trustees were the three defendants. Jeremiah took control of the £1012 coming out of her father's estate in 1846 and kept it for himself. When Mary discovered this in 1850 the Maises arranged to place £500 into the trust via a mortgage, and also offered her a coffee plantation in Jamaica but the latter was judged to be of little value and the mortgage proved to be already entailed. Jeremiah escaped [to Jersey[2]] but John Mais refused to say where he was. James Pownall M.D., responded that whilst he had been the third trustee he took a nominal role: the other two had administered it and he paid little attention to their actions, was not privy to them and simply signed things when needed. He said he would accept the direction of the court and asked that as he did not participate in the breaches of trust that his legal costs be paid from the estate.

Unfortunately for James the Court of Chancery was infamous for its slow and expensive process, well recounted in Charles Dicken's *Bleak House*. It took the view that as a trustee James held some responsibility for not preventing the actions of his fellow trustees. An order was made on 21 January 1858 for James jointly with the other two executors to pay the £1012 plus interest plus the costs of the case including the plaintiff's.[3] It appears to have taken a year for the costs to be sorted.

By now he had settled into Wroughton near Swindon and was living with his wife Lucretia, sister Miss Isabel Pownall and his elderly mother-in-law Mrs Bridget Bishop.[4]

His wife gives the following account:

> Last January 12 [1859] he was greatly distressed on receiving most unexpectedly a heavy bill from a lawyer. Although co-trustee with a man who had defrauded his sister he hoped from promises and a clause in the settlement to have been exempt. The shock was great and the dread of further calls being made harassed and depressed him exceedingly.
>
> From that time trouble followed trouble and increased his painful depression. He lost energy, became physically ill, his old fancies about poison being secretly administered came on and he complained of horrible sensations about two or 3 o'clock in the morning and not being able to sleep quietly from that time. He became worse and worse, had again all the symptoms of suppressed gout and was dreadfully restless and unhappy.[5]

On the 31st March James swallowed a bottle of Chloroform in an attempt to kill himself. Dr Morris, stated to be a local Physician at the trial (but a Surgeon with a purchased M.D. from St Andrews) stated that he saw James after he had swallowed a bottle of chloroform and become insensible. He became sensible after 2 – 3 hours 'but was in a dangerous state'. The next day he said he had taken the chloroform to destroy himself having been annoyed by a friend and 'laboured under nervous excitability.'[6]

The next morning James tried to kill his mother-in-law. This is related by his defence lawyer at his later trial to show how insane he was at times of assault:

> If there was any human being for whom Dr Pownall

entertained a reverential affection it was for his mother-in-law; she was a venerable lady of 86, living with his wife and his sister, and who had received the greatest attention and courtesy from him. Yet in one of his paroxysms while left to attend the old lady – for he was an accomplished physician and widely consulted – while looking at her tongue he broke her head with a poker, and with a razor so cut her that it was only by God's mercy she was alive.[7]

James wife agreed

On the morning of April 1st an alarm was given that he had attacked my aged and beloved mother who was bleeding profusely. He had gone into her room early to enquire how she was. He was much attached to her and had most tenderly watched her night and day through a severe illness some months before. Immediately after he was excessively distressed exclaiming "I have struck her. What have I done! Will she die?" He urged his groom going for a surgeon. After this outbreak a man was constantly with him.

In the anxiety about my dear mother (who I am thankful to say is quite recovered and as well as before the attack) my poor husband's gun had been omitted to be removed. Three men were in the house and during the night and one was in the room with him.[8]

There are two accounts of the suicide attempt which give differing dates.[9] Mr Bonham a neighbour who kept a watch after the attack, states that James assaulted Mrs Bishop the morning after his chloroform overdose[10] and so took the chloroform on 31st March, but it seems surprising that he would have been allowed to enter her room alone early in the morning to examine her the day after being stuporous on Chloroform – if true it suggests the family thought the crisis had passed – certainly he was not being watched that morning so he was not prevented from getting up early to enter her room. Dr Morris would have seen him after the attack to complete the medical certificate of insanity that he signed on 2nd April.

Dr Morris stated he had seen James on the 24th March after the overdose. A week between the events makes some sense as it allows Dr Morris to ask the next day over the overdose and for the family to start to relax and return to normal routines – and suggests that he seemed better after the overdose and they assumed the crisis had passed. It is surprising that no other action had occurred in the week after the serious but uncompleted suicide.

The assault on Mrs Bishop was clearly very severe and she was lucky to survive. The neighbour Mr Bonham came over and a local surgeon Mr Gay was summoned.[11]

Bonham and Gay agreed to stay and sit up alternately with James through the night. The two men appear to have supervised James whilst the family arranged his rapid readmission to Northwood Asylum under Dr Davey. There was no telegraph or phone system, to arrange speedy messaging though the nearby railway may have helped.

Given it is forty miles between Wroughton and Northwood House, it would have taken at least eight hours to ride to Northwoods and bring a carriage back but it was probably possible to arrange in one day. Mr Bonham states it was during the night of 1st April that:[12]

> Dr Davey's son and a keeper came to the house; I requested them to go away and come in the morning. When I went back to Dr Pownall's bedroom I found he had overheard what had passed; he said he saw through the trickery, and he went into a long statement, complaining of the conduct of his family. He said his food was continually drugged. After Mr Davey's son and the keeper had been there he became very much excited, and frequently and anxiously asked if they were gone. About 7 o'clock in the morning Dr Pownall wanted to go downstairs to fetch some hot water. I said I would go instead; he promised me he would go out and call the servant; I left the room to speak to his sister, Miss Pownall; on turning round I saw him coming up the stairs without shoes with his arms behind his back; when he got

upstairs he moved his arms, and I saw he had a double-barrelled gun. He rushed past me and went to Mrs Bishop's door. Resistance was offered inside, the muzzle being inside. I caught him by the arms behind, and Miss Pownall, who was in front, held up the muzzle of the gun to the ceiling. One barrel I found was very heavily loaded. Two men came up and took the gun away and he was removed to Northwoods the same day [2nd April, when he is described as being desponding and incoherent on the certificates[13]].

That day he was admitted to Northwood, taken by the carriage and staff who had waited overnight. The certificates were signed by Frederick Henry Morris and John Gay junior, surgeon, who called the case one of Homicidal Mania.[14]

Again it is of note that the police were not called, despite him twice trying to murder his mother-in-law. He could have been arrested, prosecuted and then sent to a criminal lunatic ward, but clearly the family did not want this to happen and preferred a private asylum admission without publicity. If he had been charged at this point the later successful murder would not have happened.

References

1. National Archives Kew: C 15/258/B101 Britton v Mais;
2. Where he is in the 1851 Census. He died in Dieppe in 1870.
3. Order within his Broadmoor notes Berkshire Archives. D/H14/D2/2/1/230/1
4. The main sources for his 1859 illness are: Commissioners, L. Fourteenth Report of the Commissioners in Lunacy to the Lord Chancellor. (338.).London: House of Commons 1860. has long report p91-97; plus newspaper reports of his trial [longest account is Gloucestershire Chronicle 24 Dec 1859] and the magistrates' hearing on the licence of Northwoods [see Wiltshire Independent 27 October 1859]; Davey's presentation and the letter of Lucretia to the Commissioners [Glouc Archives Q/AL/46]
5. In Gloucester Archives: Q/AL/46 page 5ff. Copy of wife's account
6. Dr Morris's evidence in trial – Gloucestershire Chronicle 24 Dec 1859
7. Gloucestershire Chronicle 24 Dec 1859
8. Gloucester Archives: Q/AL/46 page 5ff. Copy of wife's account
9. Gloucestershire Chronicle 24 Dec 1859 accounts of neighbour Charles Bonham and Dr Morris
10. Gloucestershire Chronicle 24 Dec 1859 accounts of neighbour Charles Bonham
11. Gloucestershire Chronicle 24 Dec 1859 accounts of neighbour Charles Bonham – he said it was Surgeon Gale but there is no Gale registered as a surgeon – there is a family of three Surgeons in Swindon called Gay so this was probably a typographical error.
12. Mr Bonhams evidence Gloucestershire Chronicle 24 Dec 1859
13. 1860 Commissioners report p91
14. Cited in long account of Magistrate discussion – Gloucestershire Chronicle 22 October 1859.

In Northwoods Asylum

Figure 13: Northwoods Asylum

Dr Davey who took on the cure of James Pownall at Northwoods had over twenty years experience in managing insanity. Born in Portsmouth in 1812 he had been both a naval surgeon and a General Practitioner before becoming a house surgeon at Hanwell Asylum in 1839. Hanwell was then one of the largest asylums in England. He worked under the new superintendent John Conolly, who introduced non-restraint methods there, and who became a leading figure in psychiatry. Davey worked up the ranks under Connolly to be assistant medical officer. He was then approached to become the medical superintendent of a new asylum in Ceylon, and moved there in 1844 but when the colony finances necessitated ending the position he returned in 1850 to become the first medical superintendent of the female side of Colney Hatch Asylum, then the largest asylum in Europe. In addition he was in 1850 granted a licence for Vine Cottage, Norwood Green near Hanwell asylum, to receive five private patients. He took over Northwoods in 1852 after the sudden death of the original owner, Dr Henry Fox, a son of Edward Long Fox, builder of Brislington House Asylum.

Henry's death followed the stress of another series of investigations by Purnell. In 1851 the newspapers reported Purnell's accounts in the Quarter Sessions that Fox was rarely at the asylum and was *'addicted' to the old system of restraint and mechanical coercion.'* [1] After some admission certificates were found to be illegal, Purnell then went in and personally examined the certificates of all the past and present inmates and publicly reported at the next magistrates hearing that he found that 135 patients had been illegally received in the asylum, often as Mrs Hawke the female superintendent signed the documents in Henry's name. Henry was the licensed medical officer and was the person who had to sign any documents. The newspapers reported this in full.[2] The business was damned.

Fox tried to save the reputation of the Asylum. He immediately put out a series of lengthy positive adverts praising Northwoods – almost entire newspaper columns of positive extracts from the Visitors books over the previous ten years.[3] Unusually the magistrates (presumably on direction of Purnell) responded with their own advert, noting that the advertisements *"do not give the whole entries made on their respective visits"*

> The Visitors do not feel authorized to publish what has been thus omitted, but consider it their duty to state that the constant use of *mechanical restraint* has been repeatedly referred to in the entries, have also the *illegalities and irregularities in some documents.*[4]

This was all very stressful and Henry died suddenly in October 1851 when dining at Northwoods. The Coroner's jury returned a verdict of *Died by the Visitation of God,* said they thought him a wonderful man and asked that a copy of their views be sent to Purnell.[5] They clearly thought his death was caused by Purnell.

Soon after this Purnell was presented with an elaborate table (that is now in the Victoria and Albert Museum (Figure 14)) for his work as chairman of the magistrates and the asylum visitors. After the death of Fox he did not attack any private asylum with such vigour.

Figure 14: The silver urn and table presented to Purnell.

Henry's son Dr William Charles Fox inherited the asylum and soon brought in Dr James George Davey to run it and then sold the business to him, though Davey still had to rent the building from him (in a similar arrangement taken on by Ogilvie at Ridgeway House). William then retrained as a priest and became the curate for the parish.

Rather unusually the magistrates, chaired by Mr Purnell, held a lengthy public interview with Dr Davey before approving his takeover of the licence. Normally changes of proprietor were passed undisputed. The interview was due to reports of his support for clairvoyance and using mesmerism to treat patients,[6] and he had to give assurances he would not treat his patients using these techniques without written permission of the Visitors. He wrote the required letter addressed to Purnell.[7] However after this initial interview there is no evidence of the magistrates disliking his operation at Northwoods. Davey may have continued to use mesmerism in his outpatient private practice but there is no record of this.

Davey took over the lease of Northwood House Asylum in 1852 so he would not have known James from his prior admission under Dr Henry Fox. Dr Davey says that James Pownall, when well:

> … had conducted a large and first-class general practice, and, what is more, had become so highly respected by his fellow townspeople as to be chosen by them for their chief magistrate, &c.. Dr. Pownall was described to me as naturally an amiable and estimable man; but, on the other hand, when insane, as most violent, and dangerous to himself and to others. On the authority of those most intimately acquainted with Dr. Pownall, I learnt that the first indications of mental disorder in him were marked by a mistrust of his nearest relatives, and by a suspicion of their intentions in so far as his interests were concerned. He declared, after a time, that poison was mixed with his food, &c., &c.. The persistence of these delusions had resulted in

acts of violence to himself and others; he became, in fact, suicidal and homicidal. During the last attack of illness, in 1854, it was told me, he, Dr. Pownall, had shot a patient of his own in the leg when they were out together shooting; but that the Coroner's inquiry into the cause of death of the same gentleman, and into the general facts of the case, went to prove the fatal injury but a pure accident; however, there were those, I was told, who took a different view of the case....

On the arrival of my patient at Northwoods, and after reading the medical certificates, I lost no time in visiting him to ascertain his then present state. I found Dr. Pownall slightly agitated, but nothing more than this; he spoke calmly and addressed himself to me and others as became a gentleman. On prolonging my conversation, he cried, and expressed the deepest sorrow for the violence shown by him to his mother-in-law, &c. I referred to the painful circumstances of his removal from home, and begged him to give me anything he might have about him wherewith he might injure himself or others. He gave me at once two pen-knives. Dr. Pownall went on quietly and comfortably at Northwoods; he appeared, day by day, to have little or nothing the matter with him. He walked out, within a month of his arrival at Northwoods, quite unattended; he joined my family and children in their walks, and rode out with my son and myself. In fact, Dr. Pownall and I stood towards each other in the light rather of friends than anything else.[8]

The dispute over discharge

After the homicide many claimed that Davey discharged Pownall too soon, or should have sent him on leave whilst still detained as a patient. However this was still a time when the public were preoccupied with wrongful detention and patients being stopped from leaving. Proprietors could be sued for this. In the Commissioners first report of 1844 they stated:[9]

In reference to the subject of liberating patients, ... it must be added that confinement has in many cases been too far prolonged and we have not infrequently encountered a reluctance, on the part of the patient's relatives or parish officers, to remove him when he has been considered convalescent, and when in our opinion he might have been removed from the Asylum without danger.

In the same report they also talk of the difficulty of deciding when to order a patient's release because the superintendent had not done so.[10]

Without laying down any precise rule on the subject, we have assumed, as a general principle for our guidance, that wherever a man of ordinary intellect is able so to conduct himself, that he is not likely to do injury, in person or property, to himself or others, he is unfit to continue as the inmate of a Lunatic Asylum.

In judging, however, of [the] likelihood to do injury —in anticipating, in short, the future good conduct of a person who has been once insane, from the present abated state of his malady, or from his apparent recovery, there is frequently extreme difficulty and always the most serious responsibility. In some cases, insanity may have been produced by temporary causes, which being removed, little probability exists of a return of the complaint. *But the majority of cases proceed either from congenital causes, or from some organic defect in the system, inducing periodical returns of the disorder, in each of which cases there is little chance of complete cure*; [Author's emphasis]

By 1859 the main legal clauses governing discharge of provincial private patients were:

- The petitioner sending a patient in could at any time remove them except if the proprietor certified that the patient was dangerous, when the Magistrate Visitors had to authorise discharge. [11]
- Whilst on certificate a patient could be transferred to another asylum or to care as a single patient, on the authority of the petitioner, plus two Commissioners. [12]

- Whilst on certificate a patient could be sent to any place for any definite time for his health or as leave anticipating discharge, on the authority of two Visitors.[13]
- The proprietor had to send notice of recovery of any patient to his 'friends' and if not discharged by them in 14 days he had to notify the Commissioners or Visitors who could then visit and order discharge. [14]
- After discharge a patient could see the admission certificates and could also sue the proprietor for wrongful detention or failure to discharge.[15]

After discharge a patient could remain at the asylum as a 'boarder', in addition their uncertified friends or relatives could also board with them.

Dr Davey states:

> About the 17th [of May, after 6 weeks] I thought [Dr Pownall] was considerably restored, and informed his family that ere long he might safely be restored to liberty, and that the change might benefit himself. ...The family were anxious that Dr Powell should be removed, not to a private house, but to Cotonhill Asylum, Staffordshire. I believe I stated I could not give the certificate for his admission to an asylum, as I considered him sane.

He later showed the magistrates a copy of the letter he sent to Mrs Pownall on about 27 May:

> Dear Madam – I am glad to tell you that Dr Pownall appears to be fast regaining his usual state of mental health, and that therefore you may see fit, in anticipation of his return home, to make the necessary domestic arrangements for his reception at Wroughton.[16]

By this time Davey clearly felt that James Pownall was restored to health and was now sane and had to be discharged. Given he took Dr Pownall on his medical visits and found him 'composed and rational' he assumed he was completely well.[17] Davey knew that the two recent times James had become ill were related to severe stress, and that there had been several years between episodes when he was sane and had operated a successful medical practice.

By the end of his stay, James was being treated as a colleague and not a patient. From other comments it is also clear that James himself was agitating to get out of the place and Davey feared being sued by Pownall if he did not push for discharge.

Lucretia responded to Davey's notice of the need for discharge by saying she needed to consult her friends. She then wrote to Ogilvie who had clearly already been speaking to the Lunacy Commissioners about the case. He now wrote to them:

> 29th May 1859
>
> Sir,
>
> In reference to the conversation I had with Mr Gaskell [Commissioner and ex-medical superintendent of Wakefield County Asylum] and the letter I conveyed to him from Mrs Pownall, I beg to inform you that on my return home last night I found a note from her enclosing one she had just had from Dr Davey, which I think it desirable the Commissioners should see. [his note above of 27 May] …
>
> Mrs P sent me also copy of the answers she had sent or was about to send to Dr D. it is a proper one, stating that however gratifying it is to hear that Dr D. thinks so favourably of her husband, and however desirous she might naturally be to act on his suggestions, and prepare for the speedy removal of her husband, yet she feels that she owes a duty to her relatives and friends and to the public which obliges her to act under the advice of persons or on whose kindness and judgement she can rely. I am writing to advise her to write as kindly as she is always ready to do to her husband, but quite to avoid the subject of his removal. He, if he answers her, will probably press that point, and by that time she will I hope

to receive the advice and instructions of the commissioners as to her future course. The case is a peculiar one, but one in which I cannot conceive the Commissioners will find any difficulty. Mrs Pownall's address is Wroughton near Swindon. ...

G S Ogilvie[18]

Ogilvie enclosed Lucretia's account of her husband which gives an account of his past character and past episodes, as cited above. These letters were not seen by Davey or the magistrates until they were forwarded by the Commissioners.

The Commissioners public account of events published a year later, states:

> At the end of May in the same year, less than two months from the date of his admission, Dr. Pownall seems to have temporarily improved, and thereupon Dr. Davey wrote to Mrs. Pownall, urging that she should make the necessary arrangements in anticipation of her husband's return home. ... communications were thereupon made to us by Mr. Ogilvie, of Bristol, a connexion of Mrs. Pownall's, asking us to interfere.[19]

The retrospective account insinuates that James had not really recovered but had only 'temporarily improved.' In saying this they were questioning the judgement of Davey. Two days later Ogilvie wrote again to the Commissioners

June 1st 1859:

> Sir,
>
> I beg to enclose a letter I have just received from Mrs Pownall ... If I may take the liberty of making a suggestion, it would be that he might be placed at Coton Hill or some similar asylum for awhile and that if he goes on well and it should be deemed prudent and found practicable they should go together to board with some medical man or at least someone who would exercise a degree of control over him. There would be some difficulty in carrying out such an

> arrangement but I fear she will not be satisfied without looking forward to some such – it is what I suggested and recommended years ago, before any positive mischief had arisen from his unfortunate state of mind – but my own opinion now is that the upmost liberty he should have would be all that could be allowed within the walls of an asylum, in which his wife might stay with him when proper and convenient. In considering such a case however it is necessary to take into account not only what is proper and desirable, but what law, the prejudices of society, the scruples and even folly of some who have power to interfere, will render admissible.
>
> Geo S Ogilvie[20]

Ogilvie was clearly prepared to work on the edge of legality, as he had done for much of his life. The Commissioners discussed Ogilvie's ideas on the 2nd June and decided to send the information they had acquired from Ogilvie and Lucretia, in confidence to Davey for him and the visiting magistrates to see, to encourage them to send Pownall out under supervision.[21] They sent a letter to Dr Davey two days later:[22]

> The Commissioners desire that you will have the goodness to lay these papers before the Visitors of Northwoods at the earliest opportunity. They consider Dr. Pownall's case to be one of much importance, requiring from its antecedents, peculiar caution and care in dealing with it; and, having regard to those antecedent circumstances, … the Commissioners see much danger in an immediate or unconditional discharge. They are of opinion that such discharge should be preceded by a leave of absence under the 86th Section of the Act, whereby the Patient's power of self-control may be tested for some little time.

This letter is 'encouraging' the magistrates and Davey to send James on leave, still under his certificate of insanity, on probation prior to discharge. They are saying that the risks justify it. However it was not for the Commissioners to tell the Magistrates what to do and it was

Davey who would be sued for wrongful detention and not them.

Though after the event they publicly declared that Dr Pownall had made only a 'temporary improvement', this letter makes no comment on his degree of sanity or recovery. As such it does not enter a discussion of whether the threat of relapse justifies supervised discharge even if he is now sane. The law was clear that if a patient was sane they had to be released immediately and they could not gainsay this.

The letter does not contest Davey's view that Pownall was cured – they could not contest this without themselves examining him. The letter says that his safety needs to be tested for a short time and avoids any issues about legality. Their suggestion of supervision for 'a little time' is at odds with Ogilvie's recommendation of permanent incarceration.

The Magistrates visited Northwood on the 22nd June. There was an issue with the papers sent by the Commissioners as the next day the Commissioners note:[23]

> A letter was read from the Clerk to the Visitors enclosing copy Resolution in reply to former communication from the Board to Dr Davey. Ordered that the documents desired, throwing light upon the antecedent circumstances in Dr Pownall's case be at once prepared and transmitted.

Pownall's 'sister-in-law' (presumably the wife of brother and fellow surgeon John Dommett Bishop of Calne) wrote to the Commissioners as on 6 July they directed[24]

> Mrs Bishop, to be informed of the steps, which have been taken by the Board in reference to Dr Powell's case, and of the advice they have given against his unconditional discharge. Also, to be advised to place herself in communication with the visitors of the Northwoods, and repeat to them the statements of her letter to Commissioners.

If she sent a letter to the Magistrates or Davey, it has not survived. The Magistrates returned three weeks later on the 15th July and saw the correspondence sent to the Commissioners – However only

Purnell and the visiting physician could attend on the 15th, as the second magistrate was on his way to Dublin. So there were not enough magistrates to authorise Pownall being sent on leave even if they wanted to. Given this was what the correspondence was over, and the purpose of the visit, it seems that Purnell had made his mind up before attending.

The physician who attended with Purnell was Dr Gilbert Lyon M.D. the usual Medical Visitor who was a well known figure in Bristol. He claimed a long experience in managing insanity, having been physician to the workhouse, St Peters Hospital and its Lunatic Wards for about twenty-five years.[25] In addition he was also born in Jamaica as part of a wealthy merchant family. He had a similar background to James of being sent as a child back to England for education, except he had a more expensive medical education at Edinburgh, and was the son of married British parents.[26] He was also the physician who had accompanied Purnell when visiting Ridgeway House.

When the two visited on 15th July they reported in the Visitors' book that they had read the letters of Lucretia and Ogilvie:[27]

> We considered these letters as possibly material to our investigation of this case, as the present movement of the Commissioners has evidently arisen entirely at the instigation of Mr Ogilvie. It would behove the visitors to receive with great caution any statement made by that gentleman in a matter of importance in which he was interested. He had been licensed for four years for a private asylum in this district, called Ridgeway House, and during the year from Michaelmas, 1848, to Michaelmas, 1849, reports of the visitors of such asylum respecting the illegal detention by him of two of his patients were laid before the court, and ordered by it to be printed. The nature of those reports thus made public fully warrants our statement. He ultimately declined to apply for a renewal of his license. On the 22nd of June last we made a special visit to this house, and examined Dr Pownall at great length. We ascertained that Mr Ogilvie and he (Pownall) had married two sisters,

that he had been formerly an apprentice and subsequently a partner with Mr Ogilvie in his general practice, as also in the keeping of a private licensed asylum in Calne. That he had purchased Mr Ogilvie's share in the practice and his interest in the house, which was subsequently licensed for himself. We clearly ascertained, though with great reluctance, that Mr Ogilvie and himself were not on terms of cordiality, and it is quite evident to us from other sources of information that Mr Ogilvie has a complete ascendancy over the females of Dr Pownall family, with his wife and his sister, and that he has an earnest desire, with a strong suspicion on our part of interest, to have Dr Pownall shut up in a lunatic asylum.

The fact against Dr Pownall, from the examination and papers, appears to be the assault which he committed five years ago upon one of his patients, and the assaults which he recently made upon his mother-in-law.

Dr Davey states that his degree of sanity is such as not at present to warrant his detention in a private asylum, and that he considers himself open to an action at law for his being now here. At the same time he considers him liable to recurrent paroxysms of mania when greatly excited by any peculiar circumstances. We ourselves are released from all difficulty in this case by the information of Dr Davey that Mr Ogilvie has made arrangements, with the concurrence of Mrs Pownall, for his removal to live with a medical practitioner and a proper attendant in a secluded village in this county, and that he expects he will be removed from this house tomorrow.

On the 21st July the Visitors forwarded a copy of their report to the Commissioners. The final paragraph does not state that James is being discharged from his certificate, to go to board with the doctor, but that is the only way this could happen without their permission. Davey arranged with Ogilvie and Lucretia to send Pownall to board with a doctor and an attendant.[28]

Mr Ogilvie asked why I advised an attendant to go with him

if I did not consider him to be a fit inmate of Northwoods? I replied "For the best of all reasons. Dr Pownall is at present in a state of sanity, and there is no law to justify me in his longer detention at Northwoods, but he is subject to paroxysms of his disorder. He may be well today and ill tomorrow, and therefore ought never to be without the surveillance of an attendant – at least not at this time."

In Calne in 1842 the Magistrate Visitors had been supportive of Ogilvie keeping a patient who currently showed no sign of insanity but was prone to paroxysms of despondency. But this was now after the Commissioners had criticised private asylums, and after Purnell had ruined three local asylums for wrongful detention. Davey was the proprietor in the spotlight and he was nervous of keeping an apparently sane patient incarcerated, especially as the relevant patient who was keen to leave was a doctor and an ex-asylum proprietor, and so very aware of the law. The Commissioners directed he be sent out supervised but had not given a view on whether, given the risk in his history, he could be treated as insane though he was sane at the time. Such a view opened them to being sued by Pownall. As such they gave no legal justification for the supervision other than 'the antecedents'.

It is ironic that Ogilvie was being supported by the Commissioners in his view of continued detention though they had previously criticised him over the continued detention of sane patients and the accommodation of uncertified lunatics.

References

1. Bristol Times and Mirror of 4 January 1851 but a much longer and detailed description is in the Bristol Mercury of the same date.
2. Bristol Times & Mirror 5 July 1851 see also Gloucester Journal 5 July 1851 for more detailed report.
3. Gloucester Journal 19 July 1851 also in Gloucestershire Chronicle, Morning Post, Bristol Times and Bristol Mirror.
4. Gloucester Journal 23 August 1851
5. Bristol Times and Mirror 25 Oct 1851
6. See for example The Times or Evening Mail 14 Jan 1852 up to this point Dr Davey had featured frequently in the Zoist on phrenology and using mesmerism to treat patients, for example in Sri Lanka. He stopped writing about these after taking on Northwoods. Foreshadowing the future, he wrote a book in 1843: Medico-Legal Reflections on the Trial of Daniel M'Naughten, for the Murder of Mr. Drummond.
7. Gloucester Archives Q/AL 40/37 letter dated 2 Jan 1855.
8. Davey. A Case of Homicidal Mania. Journal of Mental Science, 1860: 7 (35), 49-59 quote from pages 49-51.
9. The Report of the Metropolitan Commissioners in Lunacy to the Lord Chancellor. London: Bradbury and Evans 1844. Page 176
10. The Report of the Metropolitan Commissioners in Lunacy to the Lord Chancellor. London: Bradbury and Evans 1844. Page 170-171
11. 1845 Lunacy Act 8&9 Vic. c100 section 75.
12. 1853 Act for the Regulation of the Care and Treatment of Lunatics 16&17 Vic. c96 section 19 & 20
13. Ibid Section 86
14. Ibid. section 19.
15. Ibid. section 6
16. Gloucestershire Chronicle 22 October 1859.
17. Gloucestershire Chronicle 24 Dec 1859 page 2 column f.
18. In Gloucester Archives: Q/AL/46 page 1. Copy of letter
19. 1860 Commissioners report p91-2 – emphasis added.
20. In Gloucester Archives: Q/AL/46 page 13ff. Copy of letter
21. National Archives: MH50/10 p210 dated 2 June 1859
22. 1860 Commissioners report p92. Also in Gloucestershire Chronicle 22 October 1859.
23. National Archives: MH50/10 p225 dated 23 June 1859
24. National Archives: MH50/10 p237 date 6 July 1859
25. See for example his canvas to be appointed to the Infirmary: Bristol Times & Mirror 14 January 1843 where he says he has had 8 years at St Peter's
26. His birth record is not found, but he was son of James Lyon by his second wife and is in his will. See entry for James Lyon in the UCL slave ownership website; https://www.ucl.ac.uk/lbs/person/view/2146650131 accessed 10/4/2021
27. Gloucestershire Chronicle 22 October 1859 also transcript in Gloucester Archives: Q/AL/46
28. Dr Davey evidence to magistrates Swindon Advertiser & North Wiltshire Chronicle 24 Oct 1859.

Discharge and murder

Dr Pownall was removed by Lucretia, to the care of Dr Leete at Lydney on 10th August 1859. Dr Charles Lydiat Leete was born in 1816 in Ibstock, Derbyshire,[1] obtained his MRCS in 1841 and worked in Cheddleton, Staffordshire where he married. He moved for a short time to Leek in Staffordshire, then moved to Lydney and was probably still building up his practice there.[2]

Living with Leete was his wife and a servant, Mary Ann Fryer, who slept in a servants' bedroom adjacent to that of Leete and Pownall. Leete also had a house about three miles distant, where he 'kept an epileptic patient' – his dying father-in-law. Louisa Cook, the victim, was usually a servant in this other house. She is described as a 'very inoffensive girl indeed.' She visited Leete's house occasionally and so had met Dr Pownall.[3] At the inquest it is stated that Louisa was fifteen years old, and the only child of poor but respectable parents living at Halmore, near Berkeley.[4] She was indeed born in 1844, the only child of James Cook an elderly mariner and Sarah his wife.[5]

At the trial Dr Leete gave his view of how Dr Pownall came into his care: [6]

> I had seen Dr Pownall's brother-in-law Mr Ogilvie once or twice; I did not know Mr Ogilvie when he kept Ridgeway House Lunatic Asylum [1846-1849]. I had acquainted Mr Ogilvie with my willingness to take an insane patient who was inoffensive, and in consequence of that Dr Pownall came to live with me. I was applied to in July, but Dr Pownall did not come to me until August 10 in consequence of the difficulty of finding a suitable attendant for him. I understood that Dr Davey considered Dr Pownall was cured, but his own family were reluctant that he should leave until a suitable attendant was obtained. Mr Ogilvie and Mrs Pownall explained to me at the end of June that Dr Pownall was subject to paroxysms of suicidal insanity. I do not recollect that anything was said about homicidal insanity. I was cautioned not to allow him to

have access to firearms, razors, and drugs. ... I did not receive any suggestions, verbal or written, as to caution or care, or that led me to anticipate any paroxysm. I knew nothing of Dr Pownall but what I had heard from the family.... When it was stated that an attendant must come Mrs Leete and myself began to be alarmed, and were unwilling to receive him. Unless I had been assured Dr Pownall was entirely cured I certainly should not have received him. ...

Davey discharged Pownall as recovered. The Commissioners later protested about the discharge:[7]

> The notice of Dr. Pownall's *unconditional* discharge from Northwoods, *recovered*, by the authority of his wife, on the 10th August 1860, was forwarded to this office, signed by Dr. Davey. It was not received by us until the 15th August.

It is confusing – the Commissioners seem clear that George Ogilvie and Lucretia were frightened of his discharge yet it was Lucretia that ordered his discharge. However Ogilvie's letters suggest that Lucretia was under pressure from James to authorise his discharge and she probably was subservient to him and did not want to ruin their relationship. Davey unconditionally discharged James. He later said he saw nothing to make him not discharge him unconditionally – yet he insisted on an attendant.

As well as discharging James, Davey gave two documents to James when he left Northwoods: [8]

> At Dr. Pownall's urgent entreaty I wrote for him, and gave into his possession on leaving the house, a short certificate to the effect that he was discharged cured, i.e., was not under any legal restraint. His sensitiveness on this head was very acute, and I saw no harm, but much good, in helping to soothe his feelings, thus far; and so also it was I told the attendant, Richard Pook, *in the presence of Dr. Pownall*, in my own drawing room, that he (Dr. P.) was discharged "as a sane man;" and, not improbably, I might have added, that his (Pook's) going with the patient " *was a mere form.*" However I sent with Dr. Pownall to Mr. Leete, Surgeon, of Lydney, Gloucestershire, the following note, viz. :-

Discharge and murder

Northwoods, near Bristol, 10th August, 1859.

My Dear Sir, - I write this with the view of making you acquainted with the circumstances of Dr. Pownall's case, and with the view also of introducing you to Dr. James Pownall himself. As to the case, it was one of ordinary mania, ushered in with suspicious feelings towards others, and realizing after a time a dangerous climax of excitement. The disorder appears to have taken on a more or less temporary character. Dr. Pownall has been here some four months, and during the whole of this time has appeared free from all indications of mental disease. I consider him now quite well. The fact of there being an attendant with him is accounted for thus: the Commissioners of Lunacy some two months since advised that in case of Dr. P.'s discharge this precaution should be adopted, regard being had to the *antecedents* of my patient, i.e., Dr. Pownall.

Yours very truly,

C. Leete, Esq.   J. G. Davey

At the trial Davey said he 'gave the certificate of sanity to him in order to influence his mind hopefully and cheerfully, and put him in the best position for recovery.' And that the letter of introduction was to put Mr. Leete on his guard; referring to Dr. Pownall's antecedents.

Dr Davey does not discuss why he did not talk to Pook away from Pownall to discuss the risks and what symptoms to look out for and what to do if any arose. He did not give Pook the letter for Leete. It was found amidst Dr Pownall's papers after the murder and was never seen by Leete. However even if seen, it would not have put Leete on guard – there is no mention within the letter of any special precautions being needed, and indeed seems to reinforce the idea that the need for an attendant was not because Dr Davey had any concerns. There is no mention of a need for care with razors though Dr Davey in his paper mentions that he did not allow him access to his razors at Northfield.[9]

Dr Davey appears consistently clear – that Pownall had totally recovered, implying he could resume his normal life.

Davey sent Pownall out as fully recovered, with an attendant into a supervised setting, but does not appear to have shared his thoughts with the attendant or sent a 'discharge' note to his fellow supervising surgeon on what to look out for. We can only speculate if this was negligence or reflected practice at the time – an attendant of lower status to the doctor he was supervising not meriting information, and the private and personal information about Pownall being the territory of Lucretia to impart and not he as a doctor. Davey stated later that Ogilvie recruited Leete and it was Ogilvie's duty to give all the relevant information to Leete not Davey.

Pownall arrived a 'cured' man and took control of his situation. His wife obeyed his wishes. At the trial Dr Leete said:[10]

> I had no control over Dr Pownall; he told me the day he came he had got his certificate of cure; he was a free man, and would be under no control. Dr Pownall wrote to Mrs Powell for his razors, and Mrs Pownall wrote to me on the subject.
>
> In consequence an interview took place. Mrs Pownall brought the razors to Lydney with my approbation. I understood from Dr Pownall that he had been allowed to shave himself at Northwoods. ... [letter produced from Dr Leete to Lucretia dated 18 August which] stated he considered all precautions respecting Dr Pownall were perfectly unnecessary; that he was in the habit of shaving himself at Northwoods, and had had the use of a razor since he had been with Mr Leete.
>
> Before Dr Pownall came it was arranged he should have no money; when he came he had money, and might have bought razors. He appeared much depressed during his stay from being kept away from his home and wife.

Discharge and murder

At the trial the attendant 'Mr Richard Pooke' stated:[11]

> I was engaged by Mr Ogilvie to attend on Dr Pownall. … I accompanied Dr Pownall from Northwoods Asylum to Lydney on 10 August. I saw Dr Davey and Dr Pownall in the same room at Northwoods, and Dr Davey said "You are not particularly wanted; it is a mere form your going down to Lydney with Dr Pownall, as he is discharged as sane." I remained with Dr Pownall at Lydney a fortnight and left on the 23rd August. I slept in a room adjoining and communicating with Dr Pownall's room. Dr Pownall was disturbed at night. He shaved himself and used my razor. I was generally in the next room when he shaved. I sometimes left him alone with the razor; when he had done I asked him for it. He asked me why I did so? I told him it was my rule. I have had much experience in attending on Insane patients. Dr Pownall was not excitable during the day, but sometimes appeared low. He told me he had a great deal of trouble on his mind. I asked him what it was but he did not tell me. He dismissed me, [on the 23rd] saying he had nothing for me to do; that all the expense would come on him, and that he could not afford it.

However he was not asked at the trial if he had relayed his concerns about Pownall's mind to others before he left. No one said that he had – but he was the employee of Pownall.

Leete had interpreted Pownall's account to mean he was allowed free access to razors, not just supervised access, even though Pownall must have known that Pooke did not permit him to keep his razors. Leete denied anyone told him that Pownall was not allowed free access to razors in Northwoods. He does not appear to have asked Pooke.

The housemaid Mary Ann Fryer said at the trial [12] that Dr Pownall was quiet and kind during the time he was in the house. He usually got up early in the morning. Pownall appeared quiet and low at Dr Leete's, and talked of having things on his mind, but this was put down to his wish to return home, rather than continuing insanity.

The Murder

For three weeks Pownall lived with Dr Leete on the High Street in Lydney, on the south-west side of the old railway.[13] Leete also rented a house three miles away in Bream, planning to use it for other invalids. At this time his invalid father-in-law was staying at Bream with two man-servants and two maids. He was dying and so Leete's wife went there on the 29th August to stay with him. She was going to send back one of the lads to collect things from the house but decided to keep both men with her and send one of the maids – Louisa Cook. Her father died that night at 4am on the Tuesday 30th August.[14]

Dr Leete stated at the trial that on the evening of the 29th August Dr Pownall was alone with him and the housemaid Mary Fryer along with the visiting Louisa. [15]

> He appeared rational and sane. On the night of the 29th I returned home about 11 o'clock at night, wet and cold, and I said to Dr Pownall if he had had his supper I would have mine in the kitchen, where I was sitting at the time. He said he had had his supper. I asked him if he would have a glass of gin and water, as I meant to take one. He said no, as he had had a little already. I asked him if he would take part of my glass, and he did. I smoked for about 10 minutes that night … We then went to bed about 12 o'clock. About 4 o'clock I was called up and having no matches in my room I knocked on the prisoner's door and asked him if he had any. Dr Pownall got out of bed, found some, came into my room and lighted the candle for me. I told him it was a case of confinement for which I was summoned, and we conversed on the subject. … I left the house, and returned about 5 o'clock. Dr Pownall called to me from his room and asked "What was the nature of the case?" I told him briefly, and then went to bed.

Louisa shared the maid's bedroom. Mary Ann Fryer said that:[16]

> Louisa Cook came to the house about 6 o'clock on the evening of the 29th of August. I'm not aware that Dr Pownall spoke to her then, or at any future occasion. Dr Pownall called me and Louisa Cook next morning in the same way as he had on former occasions. About 10 minutes afterwards Louisa Cook got up and left the room. In a minute and a half afterwards I heard her cry "Oh," as if she were frightened; then there was a scuffle, and she cried "Murder." I was frightened; and in about two minutes I opened the door and looked out, but saw no one. [She left her door ajar as she quickly got dressed] Dr Pownall had his hand on the door, and opened it a little wider and looked in and said "Mary, be quick, someone has murdered her!" He was in his shirt. He left the door, and I dressed and ran downstairs out of the house.

Dr Leete said Louisa came into his bedroom to get instruments to take back to the other house.[17]

> She went out, and soon after I heard the scuffle on the landing. I jumped out of bed, opened the door, and in she rushed, exclaiming "Master he has murdered me! I shall die! I shall die!" I closed the door and bolted it. ... I found that her throat had been cut and all the important vessels were severed. I found that I could do nothing; she fainted away. I laid her down and she died immediately.

He opened the window and found Mary Ann Fryer had escaped into the road. He sent her for the police and help. He called in some passing men and six stood by Dr Pownall's door until the Police arrived and took him to the police station.

The Monmouthshire Beacon embroidered this account by adding that Louisa:[18]

> 'went into the room of a medical gentleman, who had been staying with Mr Leete, to enquire if he wanted to send to Bream. He said "are you going to Bream." She answered "yes." He said 'No, you won't' and advanced towards her

and cut her throat with a razor. The poor girl screamed, ran to her master, cried out "O master, I am killed," and fell into his arms.'

The Monmouthshire Beacon is the only paper with Louisa having such a melodramatic conversation with Pownall. It also is the only paper that adds when describing his arrest that 'when accosted on the subject he said he was bound to do something. When asked if he was ashamed, he answered "no."'

It adds that 'The feeling of Mr Leete's family can be better imagined than described,' but makes no reference to Louisa's family as though they would have no feelings of importance on the matter.

References

1. 1861 Census for him at Lydney
2. CL Leet is at Cheddington in 1851 Census, Wetley Rock, Leek in the 1855 medical directory and Lydney in 1859.
3. Leete's testimony at trial reported in Gloucestershire Chronicle 24 Dec 1859 p.2d
4. Gloucestershire Chronicle 3 Sept 1859 p5a
5. See birth certificate.
6. Leete's testimony at trial reported in Gloucestershire Chronicle 24 Dec 1859 p.2d
7. 1860 Commissioners report p94
8. Davey.. A Case of Homicidal Mania. Journal of Mental Science, 1860:7 (35), 49-59; page 52.
9. Davey Ibid p56 footnote
10. Gloucestershire Chronicle 24 Dec 1859 p.2d
11. Gloucestershire Chronicle 24 Dec 1859 p.2e
12. See her account at trial Gloucestershire Chronicle 24 Dec 1859 p.2e
13. The 1861 Census does not name the house he lives in but it appears to be on the Highstreet.
14. The details about Bream are given in The Monmouthshire Beacon 3 Sept 1859 page 4: 'Murder at Lydney'
15. Gloucestershire Chronicle 24 Dec 1859 p.2d
16. Gloucestershire Chronicle 3 Sept 1859 p5a
17. Gloucestershire Chronicle 3 Sept 1859 p5a
18. The Monmouthshire Beacon 3 Sept 1859 page 4: 'Murder at Lydney'

Arrest, trial and reactions

Sergeant Pope the arresting police officer, testified:[1]

> I found Dr Pownall's door locked and asked him twice to open it. He made no answer, and I burst it open. He was sitting very quietly on the side of the bed with only his shirt on; it was speckled with fresh blood. A razor marked with blood was on the wash-hand table. I told Dr Pownall to dress, and that it was my duty to take him into custody; he made no answer, dressed himself at once.

Pownall was taken to Gloucester Prison, where he stayed until his eventual transfer to Bethlem. A Coroner's inquest was held the evening of the murder and extensively reported in the newspapers. Pownall attended:[2]

> Dr Pownall sat during the proceedings, but hitherto had not spoken. He was sitting at the table, shaking his eyes with his hands. As soon as the witness had arrived at this part of his examination, [describing the death] without being spoken to, he looked up and said slowly and in a low, deep voice: "I can tell you. I unfortunately did it. I can hardly assign any motive. I felt I was bound to do something, and I could not resist it."

Purnell must have heard of the murder the same day it occurred. The man he had said did not justify confinement had killed someone. Immediately after the inquest he and Dr Lyons with some other Visitors visited Northwoods on the 3rd September and wrote in the books their version of events:[3]

> On arrival here this day we refer to the books, and read in the patient's book the entry made at our last visit as to the case of Dr Pownall. That unfortunate gentleman has within a few days been committed to the county prison, at Gloucester, to take his trial for the murder of a young female servant at the house where he was lodging. That entry shows

we had subjected him to a long examination and that during its progress and at its termination we felt considerable mistrust as to the actual state of his mind, and his power of continued self-control when he should come on discharge into intercourse with others.

Dr Davies opinion upon him though guarded was favourable to his immediate discharge which we then understood was to occur the following day, on the application of Mr Ogilvie upon the authority of Mrs Pownall.

They also wrote a long account of the state of all the current patients and checked all the certificates. They found an illegal certificate (the two signing doctors were in partnership) and demanded the patient be released and re-certified.

The Commissioners formally heard news of the murder on the 7th September.[4]

> Murder of Louise, Cook, by Dr Pownall, late patient at Northwood, and since residing with Mr Leete at Lydney, Gloucestershire. Correspondence relating to this murder, and a copy of Depositions at the inquest, were laid before the Board. Subject to be reconsidered on Mr Ogilvie transmitting the statement, which has been requested from him, of the circumstances attending Dr Pownall's discharge, contrary to the urgent representations of the commissioners.

The Commissioners were asked to resend to the Visitors the correspondence that they had about the case and Ogilvie asked the Board to get Pownall remanded to an asylum whilst he awaited trial:[5]

> 27th Sept: the Secretary laid before the Board further letters and statements relating to this patient; among them, a request from the Visitors of Northwoods, for copies of the papers, formally submitted to them by the Commissioners with a view to the prevention of Dr Pownall's unconditional discharge – which were directed to be sent accordingly. Mr Ogilvie attended the Board, and read a statement of the

particulars of Dr Pownall's case which he had drawn up for the Committee of Coton Hill institution, in the hope that, for the interval preceding his trial, the Secretary of State may consent to Dr Pownall's being placed in this establishment. A copy of this statement was left with the Board.

The Board appears to have done nothing to try to move Pownall before his trial.

In October, at the next quarter sessions meeting, when Davey's licence was up for renewal, Purnell read his review of the case which was variously reported in several papers. Some parts of the review that related to Lucretia's and Ogilvie's letters were not read out though they were preserved in the written report:[6]

> The Chairman read a report of the visiting justices ... The patient had not been long in the asylum, however, before he became very composed, and so early as 4 June, the secretary of the Lunacy Commissioners wrote to Dr Davey, stating that Dr. Pownall might be liberated on leave of absence, whereby his power of control might be tested. How the Commissioners' attention has been directed to the case does not appear in the report, but it seems that Dr. Pownall has a brother-in-law named Ogilvie with whom he had formally kept an Asylum near Calne. Ogilvie's influence over Dr Pownall, as well as Mrs Pownall, is stated to have been very great and the Visitors believed that it was Ogilvie's wish to keep his brother-in-law shut up. ...[7]
>
> *The Chairman*... read a report of the visiting justices, also a number of documents bearing on the case. They detailed the successive steps which were taken by the friends of Dr Pownall to procure his discharge from Northwoods Asylum, Mrs Pownall, at whose instance the Doctor had become an inmate, having threatened the medical superintendent, Dr Davey, with an action if he detained him any longer. ... [*Colonel Newman* said he had heard that the Chairman was solely to blame for his discharge, but] Dr

Pownall had clearly been discharged from the asylum on the authority of the medical superintendent.

The Chairman: And at the request of his wife. He added that having, in company with Dr Lyon, the medical visitor of the Asylum, examined Dr Pownall, he said that whatever Dr Davey might think of his state he should be sorry to discharge him….

The visiting justices were glad to find that they were relieved from all responsibility in the case, when the superintendent stated that he was liable to an action if he detained him.

Dr Lyon corroborated the Chairman's opinion that Dr Powell was not in a fit state to be discharged. One particular delusion he laboured under was that his food was tampered with; and it was evident that delusion had not left his mind, and, therefore, that he was not in a fit state to be discharged.[8]

Dr Lyon's public testimony is interesting as there is no record of it in the transcripts of the Northwood Visitor entries. Similarly whilst the magistrates' visit of 3rd September refers to their clear misgivings on the discharge being recorded in their past visits, there is no record of such misgivings in the written report of the time. They also say that Mrs Pownall was threatening to sue if Pownall was not released, when the correspondence with the Commissioners suggests virtually the opposite. They are clear though – Pownall was discharged as his wife insisted on it. She was to blame for the consequences.

Dr Davey nowhere mentions the claims of Dr Lyon that Pownall still thought his food was poisoned. He even suggests that Pownall had no such thoughts at the time of the murder:[9]

> …from particulars which had lately reached me, it seemed probable that the last attack was dissimilar to all former ones – that it had *not* been preceded by any delusions as to poison being mixed with his food, &c., and that therefore the presence of delusions in him could not have prompted [him] to the fatal act for which he had to answer.

In other words he was not deluded when he left Northwoods and did not develop delusions before he murdered.

Davey was at the Magistrates meeting to renew his licence but Pownall's case took up the whole of the public meeting as he was interrogated over his views of the case.

He is quoted by the newspapers as saying that in discharge *"in fact, he had the support of the Commissioners in Lunacy, which he felt was needful under the circumstances, as it was a very responsible matter to deal with."*[10]

Davey justified his decisions by saying that though Pownall *'had been liable for a long time past to paroxysms of mania'* he *'was during a great part of his time free from all manifestations of mental disorder.'* However with those paroxysms *'he was at no time to be considered other than a dangerous person; … He felt persuaded that one day some calamity might occur; that certainly Dr Pownall was not a man to be trusted, and that everyone would anticipate, knowing him, that some fatality might happen to him.'* However Davey's management was based on the fact that in all past episodes the illness started with active delusions of poison, when one could intervene.[11]

Purnell then gave Davey an escape from being held responsible:

> *The Chairman:* Then when giving the certificate which you did that he was cured you believed that at any future time when the disease was likely to bring on any amount of insanity, there will be such premonition of the symptoms that care might easily be taken to prevent violence!
>
> *Dr Davey:* most certainly; and this was shown by the advice I gave to his friends at that time. I said "if he returns home look out for any delusion, and directly you see he is under delusion place him under restraint."

Davey also explained why there were no warning signs of delusions this time - the disease had suddenly changed and the attack occurred with no prior warning signs:[12]

The disease, then, anterior to this period, had been of the ordinary character of mania, but now it had taken the character of what is called "impulsive mania;" it comes on quickly, unaccompanied by premonitory symptoms; and it lasts until the impulsive feeling is gratified, and some act is committed by the patient by which he is, as it were, morbidly satisfied, and directly the patient is satisfied, the mental health is restored.

Davey does not address Dr Lyons views that James clearly remained deluded, given at the same meeting and no one asked him about Lyon's view. No one else in all the documentation corroborates that Davey warned them to look out for delusions and act fast. Dr Leete certainly was not told this. However Ogilvie and Lucretia were not asked to testify or report that delusions had happened and Ogilvie's account for Coton Hill asylum has not survived.

The meeting concluded with Davey absolving Purnell of any responsibility.[13]

> Colonel Newman referred to the statement to which he had previously directed attention, that Dr Pownall had been discharged from Northwoods by direction of the County Chairman. Of course, Dr Davey could contradict that assertion.
>
> Dr Davey replied, that he believed the medical visitor (Dr Lyon), and the visiting justices refused to enter upon the case at all; the whole responsibility therefore fell upon himself with the Commissioners in Lunacy.
>
> The Chairman said they did not refuse to enter upon the responsibility, but we are glad to be relieved of it in consequence of the action of Mrs Pownall.

His licence was renewed.

This was reported in the press and the Commissioners immediately challenged Davey. [14]

> 3 Nov: Report of proceedings at Gloucester Quarter Sessions in "Bristol Times" read before Board, so far as

related to the imputed responsibility of Commissioners in the discharge of this patient. Ordered that a letter be addressed to Dr Davey, enquiring if he had stated at the Sessions that "he had the support of the Commissioners in Lunacy" also that "the whole responsibility of Dr Pownall's discharge fell upon himself with the Commissioners in Lunacy.

Davey later published his response to them:[15]

> Northwoods, Bristol, 5th November, 1859
>
> Sir, - In reply to yours of yesterday's date, which treats of the case of Dr. Pownall, I have to inform you that I have no knowledge of having myself referred to any "Act of Parliament" for justification of the discharge of the gentleman named from Northwoods; but I have said more than once that there was no law that I was aware of to justify the detention of Dr. Pownall in a licensed Asylum. Further than this, my statement is, I believe, not inaccurately reported; inasmuch as I did say that I had *virtually* the "support of the Commissioners in Lunacy," and that the visitors declining the responsibility attached to this case, it – the responsibility, such as it is, regard being had to the acts of Mr. Ogilvie and Mrs. Pownall - must be divided between the Commissioners in Lunacy and myself.
>
> The "grounds" on which I rested, and do still rest, the foregoing facts and explanations are these, viz.:-The Commissioners of Lunacy, in a letter addressed to me, bearing date 4th June, 1859, recommend only a conditional discharge of Dr. Pownall; and a conditional discharge was carried into effect by not so much myself as Mrs. Pownall and Mr. Ogilvie, and with this object, viz., to test "*the power of self-control for some little time*," to quote the words of the Letter just referred to.

The Commissioners response was to direct that a copy of their response to Purnell:[16]

> be also sent to the Home Office in order that its contents, under sanction of the Secretary of State, might be made

known to the council charged with the preparation and conduct of the prosecution against Dr Pownall.

At the Board meeting of 14 December the reply of Purnell was 'noted'.[17]

Pownall was tried for murder on 23 December 1859. It filled many columns across the country and some colonial papers.[18] The newspapers comment that James followed the trial in detail and discussed matters with his counsel. At one point he wanted to ask a witness questions himself but was told to go through his attorney *"who questioned Mr Leete with the view of showing that he was under some delusions prior to the occurrence."*[19] The defence argued that there was a complete change of James from his usual caring self – For example he loved his mother-in-law then tried to kill her. The Judge pointed out there was no motive for the killing of Louisa Cook. The jury found him not guilty of murder due to insanity and he was returned to Gloucester Gaol until his transfer to the Bethlem Criminal Lunatic wing on 9th January 1860.

The trial and related publicity revealed that when insane James had at separate times threatened his wife with a gun, tried to shoot his mother-in-law and 'accidentally' shot and killed a patient. He had hit a patient and then his mother-in-law with a poker and cut the throat of his mother-in-law and then Louisa Cook. He used a limited range of weapons but they were all deadly ones. The newspapers made no comment on how these past episodes had been managed but the public must have wondered how Dr Pownall had not been prosecuted earlier but had been discharged into the community.

All the supervising parties appear to have scrambled to cover their tracks and reputation, even with Mr Pooke saying as part of his evidence that he knew something was wrong and would not have trusted the man with razors (but not volunteering if he had told anyone of his concerns) – however he wanted to keep employed as an attendant.

Ogilvie appears to have wanted to publish his view of the events and asked the Commissioners for support:[20]

18 Jan 1860: further letter was read from Mr Ogilvie. The writer to be informed that the Commissioners retain the views of the case, and of the conduct of Dr Davey and of the Visitors of Northwoods, which has been repeatedly impressed - but with regard to any statement upon this subject which Mr Ogilvie may conceive it his duty to publish, while the Commissioners offer no opinion upon the expediency of his adopting this course, they think that any such statements should emanate only from himself.

Having said they would not contribute to anything Ogilvie published, the Commissioners themselves published a six page description of the case in their annual report released in June 1860,[21] quoting their correspondence with Davey and making it very clear that only Dr Davey was to blame. They emphasise the dangerousness of James, stating that in 1854 he broke a poker hitting Tongue's head – even though Guthrie had said at the time there was no significant injury. They state that Pownall *temporarily improved* at Northwoods and ignore Davey's view that he had completely recovered from the current bout. They then defended Ogilvie from the assertions made by Davey and Purnell:[22]

> Numerous communications have been received from Mr. Ogilvie on the subject, and also a statement, drawn up by a near relative of Dr. Pownall. These clearly show that neither Mr. Ogilvie nor Mrs. Pownall had any improper motive in opposing Dr. Pownal's liberation, but that they were solely influenced by their conviction that he was not fit to be at large, or placed anywhere without proper control. … They further show that Dr. Davey insisted on Dr. Pownall's removal, refusing to retain him at Northwoods as a "boarder," or to sanction his transfer to another Asylum, or to his being placed under any decided control; and that the arrangement ultimately carried out of placing him with Mr. Leete was forced upon them by Dr. Davey alone.

Ogilvie does not appear to have published – presumably the report of the Commissioners mollified him.

After the Commissioners report, Dr Davey presented the case at the annual meeting of the *Association of Medical Officers of Asylums and Hospitals for the Insane* [the precursor of the Royal College of Psychiatrists] on 5 July 1860.

He introduced it by saying:[23]

> [My presentation] is calculated, as I believe, to illustrate the not very enviable position we may be, under circumstances, placed in, in reference not only to the Commissioners in Lunacy, but to the public; whose servants the proprietors and superintendents of asylums, of all kinds, are to be considered.

He ends with a spirited defence of himself and an unusually open criticism of Mr Ogilvie transferring the blame to him.

> With the above facts before you, are you surprised that I feel hurt at the kind of notice taken of Dr. Pownall's case in the report which has just now appeared under the authority of the Commissioners in Lunacy? I think not.
>
> Blame is attributable to me for discharging Dr. Pownall as I did! I would ask you - Could I have detained him longer? What law would have justified me, in August of 1859, in keeping a man to all appearance sane an inmate of Northwoods, under the plea that because he had been maniacal and dangerous to himself and others in 1839-40, and in 1854, and again in the months of January, February, March, and the beginning of April in 1859, he would become so yet again? As I told the Visitors, and as they reported it to the Commissioners in Lunacy, in the entry in the Visitors' Book at Northwoods, bearing date July 15th (1859), I am still of opinion that I could not have detained Dr. Pownall legally, that to have detained him, "though liable to such recurrent paroxysms of mania" as his antecedents proved him to be, would have been to expose myself to an action-at-law, and would, too, have been unjustified by *precedent*.
>
> With the above facts before you, let me ask, was I not

justified, nay, more - required, to insist on Mrs. Pownall and her adviser (Mr Ogilvie) making arrangements for the removal of Dr. Pownall from Northwoods. Did I not right in refusing, in July and the early part of August, 1859, to certify to Dr. Pownall's insanity - as a means necessary to his being sent to another asylum? Mr. Ogilvie is, I learn, a gentleman of long and large experience in medical practice. He was for many years the proprietor of a private asylum; and has, at this time, the charge of "nervous" patients living under his roof; and on him must rest all the responsibility of *not transferring his brother-in-law to another asylum*, and of placing him with Mr. Leete; as well as of not telling Mr. Leete of Dr. Pownall's homicidal propensity when in his paroxysms of madness; and, last, but not least, *of sending Dr. Pownall his razors.*

I may add, "The arrangement ultimately carried out of placing Dr. Pownall with Mr. Leete" was the act of Mr. Ogilvie, and not, in any way, of myself. Mr. Leete was altogether unknown to me. One word more, - far be it from me to impute any improper motive, in opposing Dr. Pownall's liberation, to Mrs. Pownall and Mr. Ogilvie in this unhappy transaction, yet I must add, that however anxious they were to secure the proper control over him, (Dr. P.) that part of the arrangement and that part only which involves the hiring of an efficient attendant ("*one*," too, "*intended to have a full control or authority,*") for Dr. Pownall's security, &c., is mainly due to myself and this much is borne out in the foregoing mere statement of *facts.*

Davey seems to have some inconsistencies in this, in appointing an attendant with 'full control' over a recovered sane surgeon. However the audience were supportive of their colleague, including his old teacher and master:[24]

> Dr CONOLLY: When a patient has been received, and is very much better after coming into the asylum (a thing quite familiar to everybody), the Commissioners always cavil about the matter, and always dispute whether the

patient ought to have come at all; and superintendents feel themselves so harassed and worried, that I am perfectly certain that, although this is a most unfortunate instance of Dr. Davey's, such things are taking place all over the country every month, and patients are discharged prematurely and improperly. … This is one of the many evils which I think we are suffering from; and I have no doubt it led my esteemed friend Dr. Davey - than whom a better man does not breathe in the world - to be uneasy at detaining Dr. Pownall. The fact is very lamentable, and we cannot but feel for a suffering brother under these circumstances.

The PRESIDENT: I think we can all see after the event, that it would have been very desirable if Dr. Davey had not discharged Dr. Pownall, but we must all feel that such an accident might have occurred under the advice of any one of us. ….

Dr. HOOD: I wish to be allowed to add my voice of sympathy to that which has been already expressed for my old friend and late colleague Dr. Davey; and perhaps I may be permitted to do so from the fact that Dr. Pownall has been placed under my care since the sad catastrophe to which Dr. Davey has alluded; and I must confess from that time up to the present, although I have watched him with no ordinary care, and though I should say he was a man of weak mind, I do not know that I could attach any particular symptom of insanity to him. And supposing he was a private patient in my asylum, and the Commissioners in Lunacy asked me why I detained him, I do not know that I could give any definite reason for it. (Hear, hear.)…

After giving his talk on the 5th July Davey must have then realised it would be published and he should obtain permission to quote the material used. He wrote to the Commissioners:[25]

22 Aug 1860: a letter was read from Dr Davey, asking for permission to publish the communications he had received from commissioners, respecting this case – permission to be given, with limitation that no enclosures transmitted

with such communications are to be published without consent first obtained from the writers.

We do not know if he had to amend his talk before it was published in the October edition of the *Journal of Mental Science*.

The Commissioners change their policy

The Commissioners presented the shorter case of James Moore[26] in the same annual report that they related the case of Dr Pownall. Moore was convicted of assault but once in prison became clearly insane with bizarre delusions and was transferred with the required authority of the Secretary of State, to Hoxton House [which the Commissioners had criticised heavily earlier in the same report]. After a month he became calm and his wife petitioned for his discharge. The Medical Superintendent Dr Dixon asked the Commissioners to sanction an application to the Secretary of State for a month's trial leave. They told him they did not get involved in such matters and so Dixon applied direct to the Secretary of State and he approved an unconditional discharge. Two weeks after his release, James Moore cut off the head of his wife. He was found not guilty due to insanity. The Commissioners state they admonished Dr Dixon. Politically they could not admonish the Secretary of State but publicly suggested in future he demand to see more information when considering such requests before making his decision on release, 'a course which we have the satisfaction of knowing is now taken.' [27] These should include the committal papers, an account of the case and recent Case book entries.

The Commissioners also included a letter to the Secretary of State setting out their role in guiding the Secretary on the discharge of patients after recovering from a murderous bout of insanity. In it they stood back from taking any responsibility for decisions about liberation:[28]

> The Commissioners in Lunacy, feeling deeply the responsibility which they undertake in advising the Secretary of State for the Home Department, upon the question of the safety and propriety of setting at large

persons detained, after acquittal on the ground of Insanity, of serious offences against life or person, are very anxious that no misunderstanding should exist as to what they conceive to be their proper province.

This, they think, should be strictly limited to an inquiry into the mental state, past and present, and the habits and conduct of the Prisoner, or Patient, as the case may be. [and not about the risks attached to release]

In their next annual report the Commissioners write at length on the advantages of discharge on leave under section 86 as they had suggested to Davey and how 'the bad effects frequently produced by unconditional discharges from Asylums, has led us to apply leave of absence very generally'.[29] However the talk is of probationary leave for the convalescent patient who has not yet had complete restoration of his senses. What they do not discuss is the continued confinement in private asylums of patients who appeared completely sane and fully recovered but were at risk of relapse in the community – such as the alcoholic or a case of intermittent psychosis such as Dr Pownall. They could not be seen to be advocating the extended detention of sane patients.

The public reaction

There is little evidence of any lengthy discussion in the press or in literature after the initial furore died down except for one curiosity:

Dr James Barry was a surgeon who rose to be the Inspector General in charge of Military Hospitals. When he died in 1865 he was found to be a woman, Margaret Anne Bulkley. The publicity made him notorious and famous in history. The first novel based on Barry's life was published in 1881[30] and has her reveal that she was once married to a medical student named James Pownall who died, leaving her pregnant and forcing her to 'unsex' and become a medical student. There was no truth in this. However, the idea that a travesty of a Victorian virtuous woman married a physician with the same name as a murdering, insane doctor, fitted with the image given of her and may have suggested why she got corrupted to ignore her sex.

References

1. Gloucestershire Chronicle 3 Sept 1859 p5a
2. Gloucestershire Chronicle 3 Sept 1859 p5a
3. In Gloucester Archives: Q/AL/46 item 12. Copy of report – part quoted in Gloucestershire Chronicle 22 Oct 1859 p.6b.
4. Nat Archives: MH50/10 p286 dated 7 Sept 1859
5. Nat Archives: MH50/10 p290 dated 27 Sept 1859
6. Gloucester Archives: Q/AL/46
7. Bristol Mercury 22 Oct 1859 p6 Gloucestershire Quarter Sessions.
8. Wiltshire Independent 27 October 1859 p3e
9. Davey Ibid p54
10. Bristol Mercury 22 Oct 1859 p6 Gloucestershire Quarter Sessions
11. Dr Davey evidence to magistrates Swindon Advertiser & North Wiltshire Chronicle 24 Oct 1859.
12. Dr Davey evidence to magistrates Swindon Advertiser & North Wiltshire Chronicle 24 Oct 1859.
13. Bristol Mercury 22 Oct 1859 p6 Gloucestershire Quarter Sessions
14. Nat Archives: MH50/10 p315 dated 3 Nov 1859
15. Davey Ibid p55.
16. Nat Archives: MH50/10 p324-5.
17. Nat Archives: MH50/10 p352
18. See for example Gloucester Chronicle 24 Dec 1859 p2c Gloucester Winter Assize – oddly it is not in the Times.
19. Gloucester Chronicle 24 Dec 1859 p2c Gloucester Winter Assize
20. Nat Archives: MH50/10 p379-380
21. Commissioners, L. The Fourteenth report of the Commissioners in Lunacy to the Lord Chancellor. (338.). London: House of Commons 1860: page 91-97
22. 1860 Commissioners report p97
23. Davey ibid p49
24. Davey Ibid p57-58.
25. Nat Archives: MH50/11 p35 22 Aug 1860.
26. Commissioners, L. (1860). The Fourteenth report of the Commissioners in Lunacy to the Lord Chancellor. (338.). London: House of Commons page 90-91
27. 1860 Commissioners report p90-
28. 1860 Commissioners report p156 - Appendix
29. Commissioners, L. (1861). Fifteenth Report of the Commissioners in Lunacy to the Lord Chancellor. (314.). London: House of Commons pages 66-67 and
30. Lt Col. E Roger: A Modern Sphynx. Discussed in Carmen Birkle: "So go home young ladies" Women and Medicine in Nineteenth-Century Canada. Zeitschrift für Kanada-Studien 34 (2014) 126–159. Page 138. See online http://www.kanada-studien.org/wp-content/uploads/2014/07/ZKS_2014_7_Birkle.pdf

James' Life as a Criminal Lunatic

Immediately after conviction and whilst still held in Prison, "James Pownall, Doctor of Medicine", made his will on the 27 December 1859:[1]

He left legacies to all his surviving sisters or their children:

- £800 to Mrs Hannah Pownall of Brighton who had married her cousin Revd William Pownall who then abandoned her for another woman.
- £500 to Isabella Pownall and the same to his other unmarried sister Sarah Pownall.
- £600 to be divided between the 6 children of John Britton of Corston [husband of Mary Ann Pownall]
- £600 to be divided between the children of Edward Chester Jones of 4 Stone Buildings Lincolns Inn, [the husband of Jane Lewis Pownall]

And to four friends from Wroughton:

- £200 for Mary Heighway of Wroughton – a deaf daughter of a Clergyman, of independent means.[2]
- £100 for Fanny Pavy "daughter of Mary Pavy of Elcombe Hall Wroughton" "as a small acknowledgement of the kindness I received for three years." The Pavy's were part of the gentry of the area.
- £100 to be shared between Mr Charles Bonham and Charles Haddrill, Scripture readers [Bonham had watched over James when he was ill].

And to his two executors

- £100 to George Harris of Calne [part of the Harris family that ran a bacon factory that came to dominate Calne]
- And £100 to be divided between the children of second executor Thomas Harris Redman of Overton Wilts [a Farmer who lived in Wroughton and was brother-in-law to George Harris]

The remainder of the estate was to be divided between the sisters who survived him (except Sarah).

He added at the end: "As my wife is provided for by her marriage settlement I do not make any provision for her by this my Will."[3]

The will was witnessed by four witnesses rather than the usual two – Dr Williams the medical superintendent of the Gloucestershire Lunatic Asylum; Thomas Hickes the Gaol surgeon; George Mason the governor of the Gaol and "Rob. Wilson" who is later stated to be the solicitor James asked to draw up the will.[3]

Probate was eventually granted on 22 May 1883 to Thomas Harris as surviving executor.

James appears to have tried to give his money to another to avoid it going to his wife – He sent a letter dated January 1867 to a Mary Hale, asking her to hold all monies he places in her hand so he could draw some small monies from it, and that if he died she could keep all she was given. This Mary was probably the Mary Hale living in Wroughton relaying the reminiscences of 'Granny' that he says were 'so prettily delineated by your pen'. [reproduced in Appendix]

Lucretia died before James in 1876.

The Chancery case came back though as in 1877 the trustees were again sued for the non-payment of monies. In this case the Court appointed the Official Solicitor to be guardian of James Pownall to defend the suit on his behalf. As part of this his possessions were enumerated and include a dozen boxes, including a locked box, content unknown, a medicine case, a musical box, and over 50 books.

*

Dr James Pownall was admitted to Bethlem on 9 January 1860 from Gloucester Gaol. The transfer was reported in the local papers. His Bethlem case file is available on-line.[4] The entries for him are sparse and only start six weeks after admission.

> February 28th: A considerable time has been allowed to elapse without any notice been taken of this case, in consequence of the difficulty felt at coming to a correct

conclusion, as to his State of mind. It appears that, for a considerable period, he practised in Wiltshire, as a medical practitioner, that, in consequence of his conduct recently he was placed in a private asylum, where, after remaining some months, he was discharged as recovered, though the Commissioners in Lunacy, from what they knew of his antecedents, strongly urged the impropriety of this step. He then went to Lydney to stay with a medical man there, and early one morning without the least apparent motive destroyed the life of a female domestic by cutting her throat with a razor. His conduct, whilst in the hospital has not indicated any insanity.

From this point on there is a monthly entry to say 'no change' or 'No Alteration' until it is noted on the 3 January 1861 [after the year allowed in Bethlem] that he 'was removed this day to Fisherton House'.

Fisherton House by Salisbury was a long standing private asylum operated by Dr W C Finch. At this time it was one of the largest private asylums in England with over 350 patients and held most of the criminal lunatics prior to the opening of Broadmoor.

Either Bethlem was unobservant or Fisherton experienced a recurrence of illness. Dr Lush the superintendent of Fisherton sent over a note on his transfer to Broadmoor:[5]

> Since his admission here, he has for a long time together behaved well, though captious [fault finding] and intriguing at all times.
>
> He is, however, liable to recurrent suspicions of espionage and food poisoning when his homicidal tendencies seem to be uncontrollable.
>
> He is very sly and cowardly in such instances, and once since admitted here he attacked an attendant from behind with a poker, and once attacked an old patient who was sleeping in a chair with a folio volume, beating out some of his teeth and stunning him. The first of these attacks he states to have been from political motives.

It is worth noting that James yet again used a poker to hit people. This may just show that pokers were convenient weapons kept in every domestic room and in asylums, but it may also show his modus operandi!

The case clearly attracted some concern if only amongst his family – in October 1864[6] the Home Secretary acknowledged a gentleman's letter *'representing the dangerous nature of the insanity of James Pownall ... and requesting that he may still be kept in such restraint as to prevent his harming himself or others.'* This was almost certainly James' brother-in-law, widower John Britton, whose wife Mary Ann Britton's court case had triggered James' fatal illness.

In December 1864 George Ogilvie wrote to the Secretary of State, Sir George Grey, saying he thought that James was looking to escape from Fisherton House. Grey wrote to Dr Finch the proprietor of Fisherton House that:[7]

> 'an apprehension is entertained that James Pownall, a Criminal Lunatic under your charge, is meditating an escape but that Sir George Grey presumes that every precaution will be taken to prevent it.'

Broadmoor Secure Hospital took its first patient on the 27th May 1863. It first admitted women then admitted men from 27th February 1864. James Pownall was transferred from Fisherton House on the 6 February 1865 as case 230. He remained there for the rest of his life, applying in vain to the Secretary of State for his release every year for the first few years.

The case notes for his first six years there are open to the public and are detailed in Appendix 3. He appears to have been mentally ill most of the time he was there and does not really fit the description of Lucretia of him as 'naturally extremely kind and generous'.

Two or three entries give the tenor of the notes:

> 4 April 1866: Has behaved tolerably well lately but continues to imagine that various women are in love with him and that he has received signs from them to this effect. The Principal Attendant of

his block says that a month or so ago when the foxhounds happened to pass in front of the windows, Pownall stated, and appeared to be under the impression that, a bagged fox had been turned down in the neighbourhood for his especial amusement. His manner is extremely conceited.

11 Feb 1869: There is very little change in this Patient. His general health at this present time is fairly good. Amuses himself chiefly by writing. Is a very early riser and says that he has always been so. A short time back he spoke of the Chaplain (Mr Burt) before the other patients in the most disrespectful manner, making use of some very coarse jokes, and on the Principal Attendant interfering he became very much excited. Is as fond of finding fault as ever, and still has a most wonderful opinion of himself.

25 Feb 1871: Very restless and irritable lately; seems to have a craving for stimulants; fancies is that there is a conspiracy to annoy him, in which the P. Atts [Principal Attendants] and Attendants take part; writes long rambling letters, which he considers models of diction, and is anxious to exhibit them; complained, with great appearance of earnestness of the feathers of his canary having been clipped and pulled out, insinuating that two patients, Betts and Stone, were the perpetrators, but it is stated that he was seen doing it himself; When he has a complaint to make, studies the manner of it for effect.

All through his time he had intermittent heart problems with an irregular pulse and seems to have had a chronic slowly dissecting aneurysm of the arch of the aorta, which could have caused chest pain and problems swallowing that could be interpreted at times as Dyspepsia. He describes having had this since the 1830s and it is feasible that his delusion of being poisoned might have had its roots in a very slowly dissecting aortic aneurysm, with high anxiety raising his blood pressure and aggravating his aneurysm. Before the advent of treatment with penicillin long term syphilis was a common cause of thoracic aortic aneurysms. Pownall's later personality could fit that of neurosyphilis but he showed no other neurological features so syphilis cannot be proven or completely ruled out.

James Pownall's Death

James died on 11 December 1882 at the age of 75 from the aortic aneurysm rupturing – a sudden but painful death. The post mortem[8] noted he had been in bad health for two years and suffered a good deal from his heart. He was 5ft 8¼ inches tall.

His brain was abnormally shrunken with extensive atheromatous deposits in blood vessels of the heart and brain. He had probably developed atherosclerotic dementia before he died.

The validity of his will was queried by the Treasury but Surgeon Hickes was emphatic that Pownall was able to validly make a will[9] and that he *was the subject of a homicidal mania but that otherwise he was perfectly sane,* and with the notably expert witnesses to the will it was difficult to set it aside. It was carried out.

Presumably related to this, a letter dated 28 April 1883 (presumably from the Medical Superintendent and answering the extent of his insanity) recounts the murder as due to mental disease with a belief that he had been poisoned, and that it occurred after a sleepless night. It adds that 'this delusion respecting the poisoning of his food continued in existence the whole of the time he was here and on more than one occasion he attempted to do injury to me in the belief that I had been the agent in giving him the supposed poison.'[10]

His estate was sold and distributed mainly to his siblings. The final aftermath of his death was the sale in July 1883 of Northfield House with its 'beautiful Archery and Tennis Lawns' to a Mr Henly for £1790.[11]

> WILTSHIRE
> CALNE
> *FOR SALE BY AUCTION*
> "NORTHFIELD HOUSE"
> A CHARMING
> FREEHOLD FAMILY RESIDENCE
> Of the most massive character, with beautiful Archery and Tennis Lawns, ornamented by choice Trees and Shrubs, and nicely sheltered, extensive and productive Walled Garden, with Potting and other Houses;
> Adjoining thereto is a productive PIECE of rich ARABLE or PASTURE LAND, walled in, containing about 1a 1r 0p;
> Also at a convenient distance from the Residence are capital STABLES with Loose Boxes and Lofts over, Double Carriage House, Harness Room, large Washing Shed, Piggeries, Fowl Houses &c, with extensive and conveniently arranged Yard, approached from the main Street.
> The whole of the above is in the occupation of Mrs Ross, as yearly tenant.
>   Part of advert in *Wiltshire & Gloucestershire Standard* 14 July 1883

The lives of the other Players

George Ogilvie had moved to live in Merrywood Hall in Bristol, working as a surgeon with a single lunatic and other 'boarders' as added income.

Under the new 1853 Lunacy Amendment Act he could take ex-patients as boarders only if the Commissioners agreed. It was presumably on this basis that in 1854 he applied to the Commissioners for 'dispensation' for patients Poole and Tinker but was told they had to be visited by the Commissioners before this could be granted.

He brought at least three patients with him from Ridgeway. Rachel Hardy, died at Merrywood Hall in 1860 aged 85.[12] She appears to have been kept as a boarder.

Ogilvie is noted in the 1861 Census with four 'Boarders' living with him at Merrywood Hall, along with his two unmarried daughters and Lucretia Pownall. Two patients from Ridgeway were still with him: Dinah Stokes and Richard Poole.

Ogilvie clearly felt vindicated in his concerns about Pownall and wanted to publish in the popular press about it. Part of this must about been about Purnell's actions at Ridgeway House as the Commissioners note:[13]

> 24 Nov 1859: a further letter was read from Mr Ogilvie. Copies of the documents applied for to be sent to him, but the same answer as before to be made to his repetition of his request in reference to his former proprietorship of Ridgeway House.

Ogilvie may have been mollified by the annual report of the Commissioners and their public support of him, and did not publish anything, but his collection of boarders and uncertified patients kept him in trouble with the authorities.

In April 1861 the Commissioners wrote to Ogilvie about a patient who had been transferred from Longwood House Asylum to him as a boarder:[14]

> informing him that the Board are satisfied that, when Mr Baker was taken to Merrywood Hall, he was in such a state, as could have left little doubt in the mind of a person of Dr Ogilvie's experience that he was insane, and that by his reception he was violating the law. In the event of any future infraction of the law, the Board will not fail to enforce its provisions.'

Ogilvie continued to have single certified patients alongside the boarders and sent in the relevant notification to the Commissioners.

> 25 July 1861: Re Henry John Traal: a notice with respect to this gentleman, …was sent by Dr Ogilvie, wherein it was

stated that he was residing in his own house, under the treatment of Dr Ogilvie, a letter to the latter was ordered stating that as the patient resided in his own house, he was not within the jurisdiction of the Commissioners. The notice to be returned at the same time.[15]

Ogilvie must have found ironic that the Commissioners were telling him he did not need to certify a patient as he officially lived in his own accommodation! One suspects this was part of Merrywood Hall as its seems to have been split into two houses.[16] Richard Poole continued as the single certified lunatic living with Ogilvie but the commissioners who had to visit him obviously used the occasion to have a nose about and meet the other 'boarders'.

> 24 Sept 1862: Single patients: [Following examination of Poole communications were directed to Dr Ogilive] as to other alleged weak minded or insane persons detained in the same house without being on certificates.[17]
>
> 12 Nov 1862: [on reading his reply in reference to the report] as to the alleged weak minded, inmates of his house, the matter was referred to [named commissioners] to consider the propriety of a special visit being paid to Mr Ogilvie's house. [later agreed to arrange visit when Commissioners next in area, and not order an urgent visit][18]

Despite all the huffing and puffing of the Commissioners George Ogilvie was never prosecuted by them.

George eventually retired to Redland Green prior to his death on 10th July 1868. Given a brief reference to him at Redland Green in the 1850s he probably bought a house there when he first moved to Bristol but then rented it out. The contents of his house at Redland Green were auctioned over two days in October, including several hundred books.[19] His probate grant valued his estate at over £7000 but his will dates from 1836 and simply gave his estate equally to his three children.

James' wife **Lucretia Pownall** lived with George Ogilvie whilst he was alive. Lucretia must have felt some responsibility for the murder as she would have provided James with the razor he used in the murder but her thoughts and views are not reported.

She probably had little income after 1860. In 1865 she asked the home secretary, Sir George Grey to get a bank to pay her the interest on her husband's investments but he said he could not do so as the property had not been forfeited to the crown as he was acquitted on the ground of insanity. [20]

In June 1866 a petition in Lunacy was taken out to be served on Pownall, to obtain his monies in the London and Westminster Banking Company in the name of the Accountant General of the Court of Chancery for the benefit of his wife. There were however delays in serving the papers as the Superintendent was reluctant to allow it. In 1868 it is suggested by the Lunacy Commissioners [Liddell] that the best course of action is to ask the wife to apply for a commission *de Lunatico Inquirendo*. She does not appear to have done this – possibly as the cost was too much.

After George died Lucretia lived in Bristol in 6 Pembroke Villas, with George's unmarried daughter Mary, with Mr Traal now staying with them, presumably boarded as a single Lunatic or nervous person for additional income but called a 'friend'. She died in 1876, before her husband, and was buried with her family in Calne, where she grew up.

*

James' sister Isabella moved to live with one of her own sisters and then in 1864 married a Swiss doctor, Marc Auguste Berney in London, and moved with him back to Vaux (and was joined by her sister Hannah). She died in 1890, leaving an annuity for her sisters Sarah and Jane. Her will was written in England when she was staying with a son of her cousin Rebecca Bryde nee Mais again suggesting a lot of interaction between branches

*

Bridget Bishop who survived her son-in-law's attack, moved to live with her son, John Dommett Bishop in Calne where he was a General Practitioner. She died in Calne in 1869 at the grand age of ninety-six.

*

Dr. Davey continued to operate Northwoods successfully for another 15 years and his reputation and business does not appear to have suffered from the events of 1859. He served as president of the local Bristol medical societies and retired in 1875 at the age of 62 and died in 1895. In 1875 he included Pownall's case in his published reflections, defending himself further by saying people concealed from him the risk from razors and that at Northwoods Pownall would go out shooting with his son. He described his letter to Leete as containing all the facts and suggested the case showed how well a patient could conceal their insanity. Davey's medical obituary notes that he was a 'fluent and pleasant' speaker and that:[21]

> he was a practitioner somewhat of the olden type, and believed in the efficacy of old-fashioned drugs, if given in sufficient doses. He also held somewhat old-fashioned views with regard to the physiology of the central nervous system, [phrenology] but was highly esteemed by his professional brethren, especially for his social politics. He was a voluminous writer on medical, ethical, and political subjects.

Charles Leete continued to keep patients with him.[22] In 1865 he is recorded as being a General Practitioner in Llantrissant, Pontypridd.[23]

*

Louisa's parents and their views are not reported in any of the proceedings – James Cook was an older father and was aged 70 at the time of the 1861 Census, living with his younger wife Sarah in Berkeley.[24] He died soon after.

References

1. Will of James Pownall, Proved 1883 – copy in Central probate registry.
2. From census returns.
3. Berkshire Archives D/H14/D2/2/1/230/40 letter from Treasury solicitor
4. Accessible through the Museum of the Mind website. Gbor_Bethlem_CBC_04_262 to 264
5. Berkshire record Office D/H14/D2/2/1/230 letter from Lush dated 6 Feb 1865. D/1114/D2/1/1/1 folio 230 - recorded as 'Remarks from Fisherton in the Broadmoor admission notes
6. Correspondence of Home Office re prisons; to John Britton Esq of Burnham Somerset. National Archives HO13/108 p36 ref 37785 date 5 Oct 1864
7. Correspondence of Home Office re prisons National Archives HO13/108 p58 ref 37785 date 8 Dec 1864
8. D/H14/02/5/1 folio 62.
9. Berkshire Archives D/H14/D2/2/1/230/40 letter from Treasury solicitor
10. Berkshire Archives D/H14/D2/2/1/230/42
11. Wiltshire & Gloucestershire Standard 14 July 1883
12. Burial no 138 St Paul Bedminster 22 Feb 1860 Rachel Emilia Hardy of Merrywood Hall aet 85.
13. Nat Archives: MH50/10 p333
14. Nat Archives: MH50/11 p181 dated 8 April 1861 and p186 dated 13 April 1861
15. Nat Archives: MH50/11 p262 dated 25 July 1861
16. Kelly's 1863 Bristol Directory has Ogilvie and a Mr Thomas Daines Esq living at Merrywood hall. [p12]
17. Nat Archives: MH50/12 p41 dated 24 Sept 1862.
18. Nat Archives: MH50/12 p69 dated 12 Nov 1862 and p78 dated 19 Nov 1862
19. See The Western Daily Press 28 Oct 1868 p1 Sales by Auction – effects of G S Ogilvie at his late residence on Redland Green.
20. Correspondence of Home Office re prisons. National Archives HO13/108 p231 ref 37785 date 13 Dec 1865
21. *British Medical Journal* 1895; 1:621 and in Davey J.G. Reminiscences of Lunacy Practice. *J Psychol Med Ment Pathol (Lond)*. 1875;1(2):200-21.
22. He and his wife have Selena Heming a single woman aged 48 born in Lucia Jamaica as 'visitor' RG9/3978/f97, p23 household 113 - in the 1871 Census she is staying with her cousin a retired Lieutenant, in Kent
23. Medical Directory 1865 page 428
24. See 1861 Census record RG9/1749/f92p12

Reflections

This is a tragic story of conflict with no real winners. James Pownall came from Jamaica as an acknowledged but illegitimate son. He appears to have done well in England and carved himself a niche in Calne. In documents his wife comes over as rather subservient to him but that was the expected role of women at that time. She describes him as a kind man and though in Broadmoor he comes over as arrogant and preoccupied with his success with women, the fact that his sister Isabella chose to live with him and not her fellow spinster sister, suggests he was not unpleasant to live with. His life as a GP was not high status and was financially insecure with a lot of night calls and travel around the neighbourhood. Getting additional regular money from nervous lodgers was very attractive and seems to have been well supported by the local magistrates. But this brought both him and George Ogilvie into conflict with the Commissioners in Lunacy and for George Ogilvie turned his life in Bristol under the eye of Purnell into a nightmare. George gave up running a licensed asylum and turned back to having a single lunatic and several nervous boarders in Merrywood Hall a mile outside of Gloucestershire and the remit of Purnell.

We can see Ogilvie as a hero – taking in patients as voluntary patients with much more freedom than normally allowed - or perhaps as a grasping man who played the system to maximum effect despite the protests of the Commissioners.

The events leading up to the discharge and homicide and its aftermath have modern echoes. A surgeon keen to return home after bouts of insanity. An asylum doctor faced with pressure both to discharge but also not to discharge a man who is well but at unquantifiable risk of sudden violence in the future. Magistrates' views coloured by their past contact with some of the parties, and authorities shifting all blame on the discharging doctor.

Purnell Bransby Purnell is an important figure in this story. We do not know what inspired him to become such a friend of alleged lunatics but he had a hatred of private lunatic asylums that operated for profit and acted as the personal champion of many certified lunatics to a degree that led to three asylums having major changes. He saw James Pownall as one of his cases for rescue from his evil brother-in-law, and must have been shaken by the death that resulted from James' discharge.

One clear feature of events leading up to the homicide which is never acknowledged in any report is the lack of trust and cooperation between the parties involved. The Commissioners did not relate easily to the Magistrates. Purnell did not work well with Davey until after the event when they developed a form of defensive alliance. Ogilvie did not work well with Davey, Purnell or the Commissioners. Davey never seems to have spoken to Leete. Some of these barriers may have been due to the etiquette of the time but the result was a homicide and the homicide seems to have only increased defences.

If James had been prosecuted for his assaults in 1854 or the assault on his mother-in-law the homicide of 1859 would not have happened, but Lucretia and her family did not want the police involved or adverse publicity and events were covered up. What is surprising is the extent to which the Commissioners and Magistrates also covered up James' misdemeanours such as his assaults on his patients. In their reports they trumpet the prosecution of attendants for cruelty, in part to stop them being employed elsewhere. I presume they thought that as James was not going to set up another asylum after shooting Samuel Arden there was little point in publicising what had happened or in prosecuting him. Gentlemen were not prosecuted if at all possible.

Dr Davey was clear that he considered Pownall sane but prone to outbursts of violence triggered by a bout of paranoid fear. Though he was very dangerous when ill, at points when he was sane he could not be kept. He said to the magistrates that he was being threatened either by James or his wife with being sued if he did not discharge him. He even suggested at the trial that James may well have murdered when not under the influence of delusions hinting that he should have been found guilty of murder.

The visiting magistrates did not disagree with the discharge at the time but after the murder claimed that they thought Pownall still had delusions of being poisoned and so was not sane when discharged. Given there is no record of this in their report of the visit, this seems fanciful and a poor attempt to keep the reputation of the visiting physician and Purnell.

James' wife looked to George Ogilvie for support. Ogilvie was clear in his view to the Commissioners that James was dangerous due to his paroxysms and should remain continuously supervised for the rest of his life, if not permanently in an asylum. His suggestion that James and his wife lived together in a supervised setting or in an asylum was legally possible with her as a boarder but one assumes he saw James as a permanently certified lunatic, as he eventually was.

Davey several times points out that Ogilvie questioned the need for an attendant, suggesting he did not see the need for one. From Ogilvie's letters, it appears that he wanted an attendant and questioned this to challenge Davey on his views as to James' sanity and why he could not be sent on supervision.

The Commissioners wanted him sent on leave whilst certified under section 86 of the 1845 Act[1] which allowed a proprietor to send a patient to any place for any specified length of time for the benefit of his health with the written authority of two justices and the approval in writing of the person signing the original order. But they did not discuss with Davey why he considered James entirely sane and so could not remain detained under the Act to be transferred or sent on trial leave. The Magistrates avoided the matter by accepting that Mrs Pownall had discharged her husband.

We have to accept that Lucretia discharged her husband despite all her misgivings. She was clearly reluctant given her discussions with

Ogilvie and approach to the Commissioners, but once she was told he was going to leave, she cooperated rather than risk antagonising James as she was the person who had to face him once he was in the community.

Davey insisted on an attendant due to the Commissioners' instruction for a supervised trial leave, but as James was discharged there was no power to make him accept the supervision of his attendant and Davey recognised this. In addition the attendant was James' employee which rendered him powerless to control James.

Davey made a mistake in not putting the letter of introduction in the hands of the attendant, suggesting he severely misjudged James. As the letter could be read by James it was severely inadequate in what it said and would not have prevented access to razors. Davey did not talk to Leete directly and did not write to him directly by post, giving the critical information about James. However he expected there to be signs of paranoia before any attack, and this did not happen. He also stated that Ogilvie (and Lucretia) engaged Leete so it was their responsibility to give him any information.

Davey took the blame but, once Davey publicly stated that Purnell was not to blame then Purnell defended Davey's actions as reasonable and understandable at the time. The reward came afterwards as he appears to have supported Davey's practice at Northfield House, making no further criticism of it.

How the servants and the victim's family coped with the murder is never mentioned in the press – but why should their feelings be worth commenting on given their lower class?

References

1. An Act for the Regulation of the Care and Treatment of Lunatics 8&9 Vict cap 100.

Appendix 1 - George Ogilvie's patients at Northfield House

Statistical response to Commissioners 1844 (see text)

CALNE
Date of Opening: 14 May 1833

Admissions	To 1838		1839		1840		1841		1842		1843		Total		
	M	F	M	F	M	F	M	F	M	F	M	F	M	F	All
Cases	3	8	3	1	2	-	2	-	-	2	1	1	11	12	23
Readm		2											2		2
Patients	3	6	3	1	2	-	2	-	-	2	1	1	11	10	21
Discharges															
Cured/relieved	2	4	-	1	-	-	2	-	-	1	1	-	5	6	11
Not cured	-	1											-	1	1
Died		1			1		1				1		3	1	4

	1834	1835	1836	1837	1838	1839	1840	1841	1842	1843
Average number of patients	2	4	4	5	3	7	8	9	7	9
Number Deaths				1				1	1	
Number Cures	1	2	2			1		2	1	1

Forms of Insanity admitted each year.

	1839		1840		1841		1842		1843		Total		
	M	F	M	F	M	F	M	F	M	F	M	F	All
Acute mania							1		1		2		2
Ordinary Madness			1		2				1		3	1	4
Lucid Intervals	2												
Melancholia	1	1					1				1	2	3
Moral Insanity	1								1			1	1
Totals	3	1	2		2		2		5		5	10	

Acute Mania: raving madness.
Ordinary Madness: conversation or conduct absurd and irrational.

Appendix 1 - George Ogilvie's patients at Northfield House

Causes of Insanity for admissions in ten years to December 1843

	M	F	Total
Hereditary Predisposition ascertained	4	2	6
Exciting causes:			
Intemperance	4	1	5
Grief; Disappointment	1	1	2
Excessive Study; intense mental exertion	2		2
Religious anxiety and excitement	1	2	3
Bodily Disorder		3	3

The admission register and visitors reports for Northfield are in a book in the Wiltshire & Swindon Heritage Centre – A1/560/2 and record all the certified patients admissions and discharges. The following is derived from these patients' records, with the number allotted in the book for each admission. In the same book are copies of the visitors reports, but not their entries in the confidential 'Patients Book'.

In the 1844 Statistical Report of the Commissioners in Lunacy there is a return from Ogilvie that gives a standard breakdown of his patients in a proforma designed by the Commissioners. (See above and on the previous page). Causes of death given in the return have been linked with confidence to the patients below.

In addition basic genealogical research has established more details about life outside of Northfield.

Charting the admissions listed in the magistrate's book, against the return made by Ogilvie it is clear that there are discrepancies, - the main one is that the 'average number of patients' for each year seems to be closer to the number of admissions that year. It is possible that unlicensed patients were included to boost the average numbers but this seems unlikely.

THE RECORDED PATIENTS

Tracing the lives of these patients both before and after leaving Northfield, shows that whilst people having short admissions often did well after leaving, most patients, even those leaving cured, seem to have continued dependant on the support of others, often entering a series of Private Asylums. The admission numbers as shown below are not sequential due to readmissions.

Admission 1) Barbara Fussell
Admitted 30 May 1833 from Wells, Somerset. Unmarried aet 55
Adm on authority Brother James.
Bapt 1777 Mells, Somerset, daughter of James & Ann Fussell.
Previously at Kingsdown House Asylum Box - where admitted 20 Aug 1820 aet 50 from Walcot Bath, authority James Fussell brother. Removed from there 15 May 1833 not cured.
Seen as incurable by Visitors, never out on trips when visited.
Died 21 August 1837 buried Calne aet 59.
Post mortem: Inflammation of the bowels, ending in penetration and escape of the contents into the cavity of the abdomen.

Admission 2) Ann Williams
Admitted 28 March 1834 from Bath, unmarried aet 38
Adm on authority mother Ann Williams *removed* cured 27 June 1834
Clergyman's daughter. Living with widowed mother and sister Caroline in Walcot, Bath, 1841 & 1851 Censuses Living with Caroline in Walcot 1861 [no servants living in]
Died 1869
Appears to have never lived independently, but always with her family, not active in society, until she died.

Admission 3) Jane Tayler
Admitted 9 May 1835 from East Coulston, unmarried, aet 25
Adm on authority Simon Taylor father, (Yeoman)
On 22 Sept sent to visit friends much improved, on Probation
Removed cured 30 November 1835
Admission 10) Jane Tayler
Readmitted 28 September 1837 from Coulstone, unmarried aet 27

Adm on authority Simon Tayler Father
Removed 'not cured' 23 Aug 1845 [as Asylum Closed]
Transferred to Ridgeway House and is there in 1846.
Father died June 1849 – but she is not mentioned in his will so unclear how care funded after his death.
On Closure of Ridgeway House is admitted to Fisherton Asylum 17 Nov 1849 where she *died* 9 Aug 1893 – cause of death not given.

Admission 4) Harriet Taylor
Admitted 9 June 1835 from Hilmarton, unmarried, aet 21
Adm on authority father William Taylor.
31 Aug 1835 sent to friends much improved on Probation
Removed 10 June 1836
Admission 8) Harriet Taylor
Readmitted 26 June 1837 from same place aet 23 authority father
19 Dec 1837: 'convalescent and on a visit to her friends for a change of scene & not expected to return.'
Removed 19 December 1837 'relieved' then constantly under care at home
Admission 11) Harriet Taylor
Readmitted 13 April 1838 on same certificates 27 April 1843: 'on a visit to her friends for a few days past and expected back next week.
Removed 'relieved' 29 Jan 1844.
Living with parents 1851 Census in Wootton Bassett - father died 1852 and gave part of estate to provide for the care and support of Harriet.
Boarding with widow and servant, in Calne 1861 Census
Boarding with railway guard and wife in Calne 1871 Census
Died 20 Dec 1880 – buried 24 Dec 1880 at Hilmarton aet 67 – from Calne

Admission 5) Dorothy Vann
Admitted 15 Nov 1835 from Derry Hill next to Calne, married aet 53,
Adm on authority husband Simon Vann.
Removed 24 November 1835 Cured.
Dorothy nee Sparrow was wife of Simon Van Vagt/Vught/Veight - marrying in South Leith Mid Lothian, Scotland in 1807.
Their son Simon was baptised 1824 in Calne when Simon was Steward to Lord Lansdown of Bowood. He was probably still steward when his wife was admitted.

The son became a schoolteacher – there is no record of his parents later death or census record and one assumes they followed Lord Lansdown around or went to Europe.

Admission 6) Charles Butler
Admitted 1 Aug 1836 from Sutton Benger. Married surgeon aet 40,
Adm on authority Wife Harriet and brother Edward.
Removed 14 Nov 1836 relieved
Married in 1833.
In 1841 and 1851 Censuses as Surgeon/ General Practitioner in Sutton Benger, with his wife and family.
So back in practice (like James Pownall)
Died 1858 in Sutton Benger aet 62. Effects under £100.

Admission 7) Richard Gilpin
Admitted 27 Oct 1836; from Pulverback, nr Hazelbury,[Shrewsbury] Single aet 28,
Adm on authority brother Charles Gilpin,
probably transferred from Fishponds Asylum. 'previously at Dr Bompas'
Removed not cured 23 Aug 1845 as asylum closing.
He was discharged initially to Mr James Fripp at Bordeaux House, Cheltenham [not a registered asylum] as a single patient, and then returned to Northfield House as on 7 Nov 1845 it is noted he was moved from Bordeaux House to Ogilvie's in Calne and is now on register at Ridgeway House
Is a *certified patient at Ridgeway House* in 1846.
15 Nov 1849 with closure Ridgeway House admitted to Brislington House Asylum Bristol.
Discharged 19 June 1873 'not improved'

Admission 9) Mary Sophia Broxholm
Admitted 27 July 1837 from Calne. Married aet 31,
Adm on authority John Broxholm husband
Removed 26 Aug 1837.
Died November 1837.
John Broxholm Auctioneer, China dealer died 1841 and left estate in trust for the raising of his only daughter, Mary Edith Broxholm – she died 1849 – aet 15.

Admission 12) Elizabeth Tocker
Admitted 14 May 1839 from Walworth (London), Single **hat trimmer** aet 32;
Adm on authority brother Alexander Tocker.
Removed 3 Sept 1839 relieved
Readmitted: Bethlem Hospital 13 Aug 1841 – single aet 34 hat trimmer, of Kings Arch Place, Walworth
Adm on security Alex. Tocker **(Hatter)** of 11 Kings Arch Place and John Allo (Builder) of 13 Kings Arch Place.
– headaches for 3 weeks – says she has been annoyed by the neighbours, hears sounds, complains of language through the wall, Very excited. states she is seen through the wall. An Uncle insane. Discharged uncured 12 or 19 Aug 1842 not fit and uncured.
Bethlem only admitted for 1 year, then had to apply for chronic ward
Bethlem Records ARA-19 page 103 and CB-027 case 92
?discharged from Christ Church workhouse London 1 Nov 1845 at own request??

Admission 13) Richard Sisson
Admitted 3 June 1839, from Ormside House, nr Appleby, Westmoreland. Gentleman, single aet 47.
Adm on Authority Mother Mary Sisson;
previously at Bailbrook House Asylum, Bathampton.
On 17 Sept 1842 is much better, being brought back from a visit to Friends in Bristol.
On 4 October 1843 on visit to Friends.
9 Aug 1844 'still on books even though he may have been absent of visits to his friends for short periods at different intervals.'
13 May 1845: 'Out on visit to friends.'
Discharged 24 August 1845 Recovered.
Bapt Penrith 1791 Sn Mr Thomas Sisson, Mercer and Mary his wife (lately Bousfield)
1851 Census living Walcott Bath as single 'boarder' of Joseph Hulme Spry who had retired from being proprietor of Bailbrook House Asylum (where he cared for Richard)
1861 Census living as single 'boarder' with Surgeon in Cotham New Street Bristol.

Died 25 April 1863 at 2 Victoria Sq Clifton, Bristol. [a lot of doctors live on Victoria Square] Bur in Clifton aet 71.
Probate administration – estate under £1500 exec Brother William Sisson living in Switzerland at the time.

Admission 14) Richard Poole
Admitted 31 Oct 1839 from Homend [Stretton Grandison], Hereford, Single aet 22.
Adm on Authority Edward Poole, Father.
?the one man under restraint in Nov 1840.
27 April 1843 'Out on walk with attendant.'
Removed to Ridgeway House, not cured, 2 Aug 1845 to remain with Ogilvie.
Remains with Ogilvie as Boarder after Ridgeway closes.
Lives with him at Merrywood Hall during 1860's George died 1868.
1871 and 1891 Living as patient with Surgeon George Head in Portishead 'Imbecile' in 1891 Census.
Died in Portishead 9 Nov 1899 aet 82 effects £24,982
Died a wealthy man. Father a Barrister living in Homend in Stretton Grandison.
Admitted Rugby School 1826. [see their digitised registers]
Went to Brasenose College 1836, so admitted soon after graduation.
His father died in 1849 and in his will leaves money for his son James 'to make his condition more comfortable' and £200 a year for his son Richard including £100 a year from estates in Durham and York – so two of his sons needed care.

Admission 15) Joseph Stapleton
Admitted 29 Nov 1839, from Trowbridge. Age not given. Married Schoolmaster. Adm on Authority Wife Lucy Stapleton.
Discharged much relieved 21 Jany 1841.
Joseph born 1791 in Colchester
Baptist – married Lucy Ryland Salisbury 1813 when a 'Clothier'
Wife born in Trowbridge – non-conformist
1830 Pigot Directory – running school in Trowbridge but also listed under woolbrokers.
Son Joseph W Stapleton is Surgeon in Trowbridge in 1841

In 1841 Joseph not found - Wife living with her son Joseph.
May be one of three staying with housekeeper in Salisbury Square, St Brides London
Wife died in 1843 in Trowbridge
1851 Census is widower librarian, visitor with a Printer in Bath
In 1861 is widower, the librarian for the Bath Literary Institute
In 1871 a widower Librarian
Died 1 Nov 1877 Bath 'Gentleman' Effects under £20 [Probate registry]

Admission 16) Charles Awdry
Admitted 13 Jan 1840 from Chippenham. Single, Cleric aet 55;
Adm on Authority Nephew West Awdry.
Died 5 May 1840. From exhaustion and debility [no postmortem]
Has several clergy in family,
Probate Prerogative Court Canterbury – of the Paddocks, Cheltenham. clearly wealthy leaves over £4500.

Admission 17) John Beddoe
Admitted 15 April 1840 from Bristol, single aet 46;
Adm on authority brother Thomas Albert Beddoe
14 Dec 1842: 'Mr Beddow appears to the Visitors to be free from any signs of insanity, but they understand that he is subject to paroxysms of Despondency which in their opinion render it desirable that he should continue under medical care.'
27 April 1843 'out for a walk, returned before end of Visit.'
Removed cured 29 July 1843
29 Nov 1846 *Admitted* Ridgeway House under Ogilvie
Escaped 2 June 1847 brought back 8 June [lunacy adm reg no2593]
26 June 1850 admitted Longwood Asylum Long Ashton, under Dr Rogers
Discharged 27 Sept 1854 'Relieved'
Probably buried Bristol 26 Jan 1856 aet 61 – died 20 Jan 1861 at Steeple Langford, aged 61, Mr John Beddoe formerly of Portland Square. [*Bristol Mercury* 2 Feb] This probably means he was admitted to Fisherton House Asylum which is based there.

Admission 18) Isaac Spencer
Admitted 4 May 1841 from Derby. Single Bookkeeper aet 25;

Adm on authority brother John Spencer.
Removed cured 11 May 1841.
Cannot be confidently traced – not recorded as readmitted to an asylum

Admission 19) John Edwin Biscoe
Adm 17 Sept 1841 from Bathford, Bath. Single university student aet 18;
Adm on authority F B [or T B] Biscoe, Uncle.
Died at Northfield 18 Nov 1841 and buried at Calne.
Postmortem: Cause death Pleurisy
Born in Culcutta, India. Father John Vincent Biscoe, Judge in East India Company.

Admission 20) Maria Gale
Admitted 1 June 1842 from Calne. Single Servant aet 28,
On authority Mrs Roberts, Mistress.
Removed cured 21 June 1842.
Cannot be confidently traced outside of Northfield House.
May have returned to service with Mrs Roberts, given she paid.

Admission 21) Eliza White
Admitted 25 June 1842 from Tomaszon, Poland. Single aet 37,
Adm on authority brother William White.
14 Dec 1842: 'appears quite well & Mr Ogilvie reports she is to be removed at Christmas'
28 Feb 1844 'out on a ride'
Removed cured 1 Oct 1844.
Cannot be confidently traced outside of asylum.

Admission 22) John St Vincent Bowen.
Admitted 24 Oct 1843, from Clifton, Bristol. Married Clergyman, aet 43.
Adm on Authority wife Dorothy Bowen.
Died 16 Dec 1843
Postmortem: cause of death Convulsions, occurring is a state of exhaustion and debility.
Will proved Prerogative Court Canterbury: Clerk of Highclere, dated 1838 – clearly wealthy with multiple estates

Admission 23) Sarah Pickett
Admitted 30 Dec 1843 from Wroughton, single aet 45;
Adm on authority Samuel Ballard Pickett, father
[James Pownall provides second certificate so cannot be in partnership with George]
Died 9 Jany 1844 'after 3 weeks distressing and painful illness'

Admission 24) Edward Scriven
Admitted 10 Jany 1844 from Kensington- single 'In the Bank of England' aet 27;
Adm on authority Mother Joanna Elizabeth Scriven.
Removed Relieved 11 Oct 1844
Cannot be confidently traced afterwards
Born 1816 St Pancras son of Edward and Joanna Scriven –
His father an Artist in 1841 Census –
See Wikipedia entry for *father – famous engraver*. Father died 1841

Admission 25) Jane Daubeny
Admitted 21 Jan 1845 from Seend, Wilts.; Single aet 19;
Adm on authority G W Daubeny, Father.
Discharged 21 Sept 1845 Recovered.
Father is the vicar of Seend.
Jane is living with him in 1851 Census just prior to adm.
Then appears to have been admitted to a succession of asylums
Brislington house Adm 28 June 1851 disch 2 Aug 1851 recovered
Sandywell Park, Cheltenham adm 19 Dec 1854
disch 18 May 1855 Recovered
Sandywell Park, Cheltenham adm 23 Jan 1857
Disch 12 June 1857 Recovered
Then living with mother in Seend in 1861 Census
Amberd House, Nr Taunton adm 6 Apr 1865 *disch* 29 June 1866 Relieved
Northwoods, Frampton Cotterell Adm 26 July 1866 *Disch* 29 Apr 1869 Relieved
Bailbrook House, Bathampton Adm 29 Apr 1869 Disch 10 Sept 1877 *Recovered*
Living with a ?medical family by Ledbury in 1881 Census when stated to be a Lunatic Patient. Appears to have *died* in Mansfield area 1884.

Boarders:
Only one of the Boarders is known by name:
August 1843: - **Mr Sissons**. Is mistakenly said to be a boarder.

Mr T C Hayward: 9 August 1844 boarder: 'a gentleman who has been a certified patient in two different asylums.'
6 Feb 1845: 'Still a Boarder, gone out for a while.'
13 May 1845: 'has quitted house and now is resident at a cottage in the neighbourhood'
This man was the subject of Purnell's enquiry at Ridgeway.

9 August 1844 Two other boarders in House. – have left by 6 Feb 1845.

Appendix 2
James Pownall's Patients at Northfield House

The 1851 Census is a snapshot of his patients before he was licensed to have any:

1851 Census: Northfield House, Curzon Street, Calne

Name	Relation	Condition	Age	Occupation	Where born
James Pownall	Head	Marr	43	Practicing Surgeon MRCS & LAS	Jamaica
Lucretia Pownall	Wife	Marr	42		Calne
Samuel Chapman	Patient	Unm	50	Formerly a Farmer	Semington Wilts
Samuel Arden	Patient	Unm	33	Lieut – retired EICS	India
John F Wansbrough	Patient	Unm	51	Annuitant	Salisbury
Richard Tongue	Patient	Unm	56	Amateur Artist	Bath
Eliza Grimes	Patient	Unm	24	not stated	Gomersal Yorks
Mary Gould	Servt	Unm	32	Cook	Merriott Somst
Mary Bolsam	Servt	Unm	22	House servant	Tiverton Devon
Jesse Taylor	Servt	Unm	22	Groom	Calne

Source: *Nat Archives: HO107/1837/folio 71 page 28.*

The fact he had a groom indicates some wealth but it was vital that he had a coach if he was to go and collect patients or take patients out on trips or to visit their relatives. Given there are no male attendants one assumes the Groom had many roles.

His known patients:
Henry Crook Pinneger
Born 1810 Compton Bassett, (by Calne) son of John Pinneger Farmer
Part of a well established local family.
Adm 20 Dec 1846 to Ridgeway House
Discharged 22 Jan 1847 Recovered

Admitted to Northfield as an uncertified patient or single lunatic
May 1847 escaped and 'parties had encouraged escape'.

1871 Census – greengrocer in Swansea
1874 as a bachelor grocer, marries a widow in Swansea.
1877 died in Swansea

Samuel Chapman
In 1851 Census at Northfield House: Unmarried aged 50
Formerly a Farmer born Semington Wilts apparently not a certified patient
Burr Holt, Wiltshire 28 June 1851 – Samuel Chapman from Calne [c]
Was reported to Commissioners as a suicide by nearby Proprietor but no record in newspapers of any coroner's inquest

Eliza Grimes
In 1851 Census at Northfield House, Unmarried aged 24
occupation not stated born Gomersal Yorks
Not in Central Lunacy register at Northfield but
Admitted York Hospital 10 Apr 1855 where she *died 1887* [a]

Thomas Richard Besant
(1) first certified patient *admitted 9 July 1852*
From Dorchester, aged 15½ Single, sent by father
Transferred 'relieved' 6 July 1854 to The Grove asylum, Catton nr Norwich [a]

Born circa 1837? Baptised 1841 Lucknow, Bengal.
1851 Census: with family & nurse in Dorchester. Son of captain in East India Company
Presume admitted informally to Northfield during 1851-2
Discharged from the Grove asylum 1 Mar 1879 not improved
Father died 1874 with estate valued under £600
appears to be *transferred to* Norfolk Co Asylum (as a pauper patient) as money ran out.
there in 1891 and *died there 1904*

Samuel Arden
In 1851 Census at Northfield House: Unmarried aged 33
Lieut – retired East India Company born India
(2) admitted 9 July 1852.from Turley, Lichfield, aet 34.
Sent by sister Eliza Jane Bass [wife of Michael Thomas Bass M.P.]
Who lived in Turley - The Ardens said to be of Longroft Hall, Staffordshire
Shot by Pownall 22 June 1854 and died next morning.
Born India about 1817
1830 appointed Lieutenant Bengal Army – retired 1839

Jemima Catherine Verenne
(3) *Admitted* as certified patient Northfield House 10 July 1852
From Bath aet 56, widow,
sent by daughter Matilda Pargeter
Discharged recovered 26[a] or 29 March 1853 [records disagree]
Born 1796 in Elm, Cambridgeshire dau George Varenne
married 1816 Joseph Gill rector of Staplehurst Kent.
husband took her name by Royal Licence.
In Bath Directory 1846 [Widow]
In *1851 Census* visitor at a boarding house in Marylebone (where others called inmates)
18 July 1854 issued with a passport. Probably went to Germany where daughter Matilda had child in Bonn 1854.
no record in 1861 or 1871 Census – probably with daughter abroad.
Returned to Weymouth with daughter.
Died a widow 1873 Weymouth – probate 1873 effects under £800.

John Fussell Wansbrough

In 1851 Census at Northfield House as unlicensed patient: Unmarried aged 51 Annuitant born Salisbury
(4) Admitted as certified patient 10 July 1852, Ridgeway House given as address.
Farmer, single,
Sent by Brother Henry Wansborough. Not noted in central register of admissions
On closure of Northfield transferred to Kingsdown House Box 10 July 1854 'relieved'
Born Shrewton by Salisbury, Wilts 1800.
1822 John Fussell grandfather of Nunney died leaving £1000 and more to grandson John Fussell Wansborough as son of his only daughter. Money to be invested in 5% trusts and dividend paid to 'the person for the time being with whom my said Grandson shall reside towards the maintenance and support of my said grandson for and during his natural life. [i.e.£50 a year] 1833 Father John Wansborough , Gent. died, in will states he is leaving nothing to his son John as he has advanced considerable sums on him already and he is provided for in his grandfathers will.
Not found in 1841 Census
Admitted Ridgeway Asylum 23 April 1847. [a] Disch relieved 10 Nov 1849 by Ogilvie as place closed. [a]
1871 listed at Kingsdown House, as 'Lunatic' as are all the patients where *died Aug 1873*
Probate Administration to brother – estate under £3000
John had a non-fatal long term condition from childhood – probably learning difficulties.

Mary Wansey

(5) Admitted as certified patient 10 July 1852 from Warminster, aet 26, Single
sent by father George Wansey.
Father baptised as a non-conformist
Discharged Improved 10 Aug 1852; 'Visitor' with Warminster family in Hackney in 1861
Born 1826 Warminster dau George & Jane Wansey. George a Clothfactor & Gent.

In 1841 Census with parents in Warminster,
1851 Census with Uncle in Sussex
1858 father died estate under £600
1861 mother died estate under £450
1861 with ?relative in Hackney as 'visitor'
1871 Boarder in Bathwick, Bath
1901 Boarder in Bridgewater
Died Single 1913 Hampshire.   Estate £1679

Richard Tongue
In *1851 Census at Northfield House,*
Patient Single aged 56 Amateur Artist
Born 1795 Bath bapt 1796 Independent chapel Bath sn Richard & Ann
(6) *Admitted* as certified patient 12 July 1852.
Sent by sister Elizabeth Tongue
Previously at Bailbrook House and Fiddington House
From Bathwick Hill, Bath, aet 57, Leather Merchant and Landscape painter.
Assaulted by James Pownall April/May 1854
Transferred to Kingsdown House Box 26 May 1854 [a]
'improved' [where *died 1873]*
In 1824 inherited a share of his father's business in leather.
Sculpting and painting from at least 1822.
Painting in 1830's
Business sold 1839 then he lived with his sisters in Bathwick.
Adm Bailbrook 1844
Adm Fiddington 1845
Died at Kingsdown House – estate under £100
[See entry in *D.N.B.*by Bernard Nurse]

Christopher Henry John Halcomb
(7) *Admitted* as certified patient 6 Nov 1853 sent by mother.
From Bishops Canning, aet 28, single, clergyman.
Disch Relieved 18 November 1853
Born London 1824   son of lawyer. Matriculated Cambridge 1845 and Curate of Guilsborough, Northamptonahire in 1851 Census.
Married 1860 in Middlesex daughter of Solicitor then went to Nelson, New

Zealand as clergyman, where family born and grew up.
Died in Nelson 1877

Sources:
Admission details from register at *Wiltshire Record Office* A1/560/2 unless stated otherwise.
[a] Lunacy Patient Admission Registers *Nat Archives* MH94 Digitised on *Ancestry.com*
[b] Patient register for Kingsdown House Asylum, Box *Wilts Record Office* A1/560/1
[c] Holt parish registers
Other details via genealogical search engines *Ancestry* or *Findmypast*.

Appendix 3 – The Broadmoor case notes for James Pownall.

The first six years of the case notes and related papers for James Pownall are open to the public.

Royal Berkshire Archives: D/H14/D2/2/1/230

Casebook: D/H14/D2/1/1/1 pg 230:

Admission [to Broadmoor 6 Feb 1865]

Remarks from Fisherton: The antecedents of this patient's case are fully detailed in the 14th annual report of the Lord Chancellor by the Commissioners in Lunacy. Since his admission here, he has for a long time together behaved well though captious and intriguing at all time.

He is however liable to recurrent suspicious of espionage and food poisoning when his homicidal tendencies seem to be uncontrollable. He's very sly and cowardly in such instances and once since admitted here he attacked an attendant from behind with a poker, and once attacked an old patient who was sleeping in a chair with a folio volume beating out some of his teeth and stunning him. The first of these attacks he states to have been from political motives.

10 Feb 1865: The substance of the Commissioners report above alluded to is that Pownall was discharged cured from a private lunatic asylum kept by doctor Davey and sent with an attendant (who however was only in the position of a servant to him) to live in the house of Mr Leete a Surgeon. A fortnight afterwards he cut the throat of a maid servant in the house. From Pownall's manner and conversation since he has been here it is evident that he is continually thinking of women.

4 July 1865: In good bodily health. Manner overbearing and conceited to a degree. A theatrical performance took place yesterday evening. Pope the principal performer, Dr Pownall made a set speech at breakfast this morning, he accused 'Pope' of turning Mr Orange [deputy supt] and Mr Burt [Chaplain] into ridicule. Some words passed between Pownall and Pope, the former said "if you are not quiet I shall put you across my knee and smack your A__" He further said that the theatricals ought to be taken out of Pope's hands and that he and Robinson ought to have the management.

6 July 1865 It came to my knowledge yesterday that [Pownall] had a bottle of Cherry Brandy in his room, the bottle was found, (a quart bottle half full) in a travelling bag, Pownall had tampered with the Scullery Attendant (Clacy) and induced the man to bring in for him this Brandy. Money to the amount of 23/- was also taken from [Pownall] and placed to his credit.

21 Nov 1865: Removed from No 2 to No 5 Block on 3 Nov in consequence of writing letters to the Supt's family and throwing them over the wall into his Garden.

4 April 1866: Has behaved tolerably well lately but continues to imagine that various women are in love with him and that he has received signs from them to this effect. The Principle Attendant of his block says that a month or so ago when the foxhounds happened to pass in front of the windows, Pownall stated, and appeared to be under the impression that, a bagged fox had been turned down in the neighbourhood for his especial amusement. His manner is extremely conceited.

7 July 1866: Out of sorts. Pulse intermits irregularly, sometimes after four and sometimes after thirty and forty regular beats. Consents to take medicine. Says that he suffered from intermittent pulse three years ago but that, since then, the pulsation has been regular. Chafes very much at Confinement.

16th July 1866: Pulse intermixed at about every fifth beat. Cardiac dullness large. Pulse slightly lagging behind first sound. Impulse of apex the left of nipple.

6th August 1866: Action of heart still very irregular. Pulse intermits continuously. Aortic regurgitant murmur? Is evidently in a most critical condition.

Is taking now Magn Sulph and Vinum Colchici

22 Aug 1866: Pulse still intermittent but less so. Has no pulse at left radial [suggesting aortic arch aneurism] Has marks of cupping over cardiac region. Says he cupped himself many years ago at Bath for Cardiac pain. [3]

25 Nov 1866: Bodily health improved, no change mental state.

20 Feb 1867: In January threatened an attendant who had offended him. He is very irritable and quarrelsome. Continually talking about women with whom according to his own account he has been very successful. After periods of excitement he remains in a semi stupid sleepy state.

27 May 1867: He wrote a letter to Dr Meyer [supt] a few days since complaining of the conduct of one of the Officers in Chapel which according to his account was highly improper. This was entirely a delusion.

24 Aug 1867: Was seen by the Council of Supervision at their meeting yesterday – His conversation and manner were markedly insane. He told the Chairman Sir W Hayter that one of the proprietors of Fisherton House had pressed him to accept the hand of his daughter which he said showed conclusively that he was considered sane there, and indeed he felt sure that there could be no doubt of that matter. He is very uneasy just now at his detention and requires careful watching.

[**Nov 1867:** Told his application to be released is refused.

30 June 1868: Chronic mania with numerous delusions.

3 Nov 1868: About a month ago he conducted himself so badly at Church that since then he has not been allowed to go. Talks very big of his former exploits, both as a huntsman and sportsman generally. His general health is fairly good. Says that

Continued D/H14/D2/1/1/2 p462:

he suffers from Dyspepsia at times and then treats himself by means of a change in diet.

11 Feb 1869: There is very little change in this Patient. His general health at this present time is fairly good. Amuses himself chiefly by writing. Is a very early riser and says that he has always been so. A short time back he spoke of the Chaplain (Mr Burt) before the other patients in the most disrespectful manner, making use of some very coarse jokes, and on the Principal Attendant interfering he became very much excited. Is as fond of finding fault as ever, and still has a most wonderful opinion of himself.

7 May 1869: There is no change in this patient. Goes out occasionally for a walk, attended by one of the principal attendants, when he takes great pains to get himself up for the occasion. Last Month he stated that Lord Lytton must have seen his (Dr Pownall's) writing for the last 12 months, and that Lord Lytton must have copied it word for word in one of his stories that appeared in the London Society.

31 Oct 1869: Is fully possessed with the idea efforts are being made in high quarters for his release; and that I (D.M.C.) had been sent by his friends on his special behoof. Betrays the muddy current of his thoughts, by constant obscene, allusions, or innuendos. Owing to his applying a small, private stock of drugs, which he was allowed, for the benefit(?) [sic] of other patients, it was arranged by order that this stock should be transferred from his possession to the charge of the Principal Attendants. Fancying that this order was due to the influence of one of the Medical Officers, he traced up a whole course of systematic ill usage, for which he said, he had to thank the same gentleman, employing violent language to increase the force of his remarks.

Appendix 3 – The Broadmoor case notes for James Pownall.

19 Jan 1870: Frequently suffers from pain connected with the head [sic] and partial syncope. These attacks of angina are more frequent after unusual mental excitement. He has been particularly restless of late and talked to one of the attendants of the air being filled with spirits around him. He is also irritable, and he imagines that other patients make sarcastic remarks about his Bagatelle playing.

5 April 1870: Has not had any attacks of heart pain lately, and seems in fair health at present. Mental condition as usual.

22 Oct 1870: Intermission of pulse troublesome again lately. Has been sent out for walks about the estate two or three times a week. Is troubled just now about monetary affairs. Rambles more than formerly in conversation.

[**29 Dec 1870:** Petition (for release) rejected]

25 Feb 1871: Very restless and irritable lately; seems to have a craving for stimulants; fancies is that there is a conspiracy to annoy him, in which the P. Atts [Principal Attendants] and Attendants take part; writes long rambling letters, which he considers models of diction, and is anxious to exhibit them; complained, with great appearance of earnestness of the feathers of his canary having been clipped and pulled out, insinuating that two patients, Betts and Stone, were the perpetrators, but it is stated that he was seen doing it himself; When he has a complaint to make, studies the manner of it for effect.

23 Oct 1871: In bed lately with Catarrh in the head and face, by which, though he recovered from the immediate effects in a day or two, he was much pulled down. Has a peculiar genius for misconstruing or perverting what is said to him – a restless genius too, being only happy in going as close as possible to the line of what is not permitted, or making work for the pacificators.

Here the case notes become closed.

Correspondence file adds:
4 June 1866: Pownall's wife served petition in Lunacy on James Pownall to

obtain a transfer of certain of his monies and later says on advice of the Lunacy Commissioners. Long delay on service and finally further correspondence stating that the opinion of Secretary Hardy is that 'the proper way of settling the money affairs of Dr Pownall would be by applying for a commission of *de lunatico inquirendo* if the estate is of sufficient value.' And that the proceedings should be instituted by the wife or a near relative. It was clearly suggested that the Solicitor of the Home Office should do this but this was firmly rejected by the Secretary of State. Nothing then seemed to happen.

1877: Further court case re Britton vs Mais. Letter asks 20 Nov 1877 that an affidavit be provided as to the service of the documents on Dr Pownall at this time an inventory of his possessions is taken which is too long for this work but apart from clothing and personal watches and chains, includes a box of medicines; a set of 4 boxing gloves, a locked cash box containing sundry letters, a telescope, bird cage and bird bath and an locked box of unknown content.

13 Nov 1880 Letter saying 'his health has failed very much of late'

25 Nov 1882 Card to say Dr Pownall is "seriously unwell"

11 Dec 1882 Card noting that he died at 4.45am with letter saying: 'a change came over him yesterday but he was clear in his conversation when I saw him in the morning and he expressed himself as being free from pain.'

13 Dec 1882 – Noted that a water cushion, small pillow and flannel cape were bought for his use about a year ago by his sister Mrs Jones and suggested they be given to her when she attends for the funeral on Friday.

He died on 11 December 1882. The postmortem noted he had been in bad health for 2 years and suffered a good deal from his heart.

He was 5ft 8¼ inches tall.

His brain was abnormal with a lateral ventricle dilated and gaping with the brain convolutions small and contracted and an effusion over the upper surface of the left hemisphere, with

Appendix 3 – The Broadmoor case notes for James Pownall.

extensive atheromatous deposits in the brain blood vessels.

His heart's blood vessels also had atheroma and four gallstones.

His lungs were small and congested with old pleural adhesions at the left base, [indicating a past infection]

He had a dissecting aneurysm at the arch of the aorta which had burst at the upper part. The whole length of the aorta contained clots which had become partially organised.

There is one example of James' writing given in the correspondence files, namely a copy of letter from Dr Pownall to Miss Mary Hale (presumably in Wroughton) dated 9 January 1867: It appears coherent though rather stilted in style, but this may reflect his more long standing style of writing.

> My dear Mary –
>
> From an expression in your note yesterday and from fresh circumstances which have crossed my mind I am most anxious that yours should be disabused. Let this note be carefully reserved in as much as the man under my present position who transacts other money matters is fully competent to manage as I intend with you and as I have commenced. Lest you should misconstrue my meaning I will endeavour to construct my intimation in the most intelligible terms. I beg you as a particular personal favour to myself to hold all monies I placed in your hands from which I can draw small sums from time to time as I may desire your intended kindness to remit it. But as I am not my own keeper and should it please our heavenly father to call me hence - whatever sums may be in your hands in that event it is my most positive desire that you should appropriate all such sums to your own use. Your friends are thorough people of business who can advise you under the circumstances should the calamity befall ere I have been of some use - before I lay me down for the last time - It is not our nature to give way to melancholy thoughts. I therefore gain in the annexed - other monies will soon drop in your hands.
>
> [Copy then adds: (There follows: 'The Woes of a Thaw' –

some verses evidently cut from a newspaper.) this is a long poem printed in several papers during January 1867 eg Oxford Journal 12 Jan 1867 p4, about the woes of experiencing a thaw with a roof damaged when cleared of snow]

I suppose we must attribute our enhanced feelings to circumstances at times, that is we at one time are under such as makes the dish more relishable. How much I enjoyed the reminiscences of Granny and Mammar so prettily delineated by your pen - not given to sentiment, eh? Who said so but your own lips. Make my kindest regards to them - I think you had better start a little banking account, then the cash will be in your name. You'll have "Faith Secular" soon and believe me my dear Mary

Sincerely yours   Jas Pownall

References

1. Commissioners, L. (1844). Statistical Appendix to the Report of the Metropolitan Commissioners in Lunacy to the Lord Chancellor. London.p144.
2. National Archives: MH50/41 entry 7 Nov 1845
3. Cupping was the treatment based on humeral theory from medieval days, where blood was drawn by scratching the skin then putting a hot cup over it so as it cooled it sucked the skin and blood. In this case it may have also provided counter irritation.
4. See Berkshire Archives D/H14/D2/2/1/230/10 ff
5. Berkshire Archives D/H14/D2/2/1/230/17
6. Berkshire Archives D/H14/D2/2/1/230/23
7. Berkshire Archives D/H14/D2/2/1/230/25
8. Berkshire Archives D/H14/02/5/1 folio 62.
9. Berkshire Archives D/H14/D2/2/1/230/1

Bibliography

Specific sources are cited in the notes for each chapter. In general the main sources for this work are:

Newspapers
- Gloucester Chronicle has extensive accounts of the inquest, trial and magistrate discussion.
- Davey (1860). A Case of Homicidal Mania. *Journal of Mental Science, 7*(35), 49-59. doi:10.1192/bjp.7.35.49 – has Davey's account of the events.

Parliamentary Papers
- The 1860 Annual report of the Commissioners in Lunacy devotes several pages to reporting this case.

Gloucester Record Office:
- QAL/46 is a collection of the letters and reports written during James Pownall's stay at Northwood House.

Wiltshire Record Office:
- Records of Calne – of Calne Borough Council, and poor law rates.
- A1/560/2 record of Admissions and Magistrate visits to Northfield asylum under Ogilvie, and admissions under Dr Pownall.

Royal Berkshire Record Office: has Dr Pownall's Case file for Broadmoor. D/H14/D2/2/1/230